SECURE THE CLOUD

AZURE NETWORKING FOR ENGINEERS

FIRST EDITION

Preface

Welcome to the **1st Edition** of *Secure the Cloud: Azure Networking for Engineers*, your practical introduction to Azure networking and cloud infrastructure design. Whether you're just starting your cloud journey or transitioning from traditional on-premises systems, this book is tailored to help you build a strong foundation in Azure networking while addressing modern security, scalability, and compliance challenges.

Azure's rapid evolution and adoption across industries necessitate a comprehensive and beginner-friendly guide that focuses on real-world applications rather than theoretical overviews. This book aims to bridge that gap by providing a clear, hands-on approach that demystifies Azure's networking stack. We've taken great care to construct a learning path that's both accessible and deep enough for technical readers preparing for certification, implementation, or migration projects.

Each chapter builds on the previous one, gradually introducing advanced topics such as hybrid networking, governance, and performance tuning. From understanding Virtual Networks (VNets) and firewalls to architecting resilient infrastructures and exploring real-world deployments, this guide balances theory, best practices, and practical examples.

Here's a glimpse of what you'll learn:

- The underlying principles and value of cloud-based networking.

- How to securely configure and manage Azure Virtual Networks and their components.

- Strategies for hybrid connectivity using VPNs and ExpressRoute.

- Techniques for optimizing performance, cost, and security.

- Lessons from enterprise and government cloud deployments.

You'll also find appendices that serve as reference material, from glossaries and sample projects to a developer-friendly API guide. Whether you're studying alone or as part of a team, this guide is meant to serve as both a learning resource and a field manual.

Let's embark on your journey to becoming confident in Azure networking.

Table of Contents

Chapter 1: Introduction to Azure Networking

Understanding Cloud Networking Paradigms

In the realm of modern IT, networking has undergone a massive transformation. Gone are the days when networking was confined to hardware switches, physical cabling, and a strict perimeter-based security model. Today, cloud networking paradigms introduce abstracted, software-defined architectures that provide flexibility, scale, and programmability.

Cloud networking refers to the practice of managing network functions, connectivity, and security in a cloud computing environment. In Azure, this is accomplished through a set of virtualized services that mimic traditional on-premises infrastructure—yet go beyond in offering scalability, automation, and integration with other cloud-native services.

Traditional vs. Cloud Networking

In traditional environments, networking relies heavily on physical devices—routers, firewalls, load balancers—interconnected in complex ways. Any modification typically requires manual intervention, downtime, and rigorous change control.

Azure cloud networking flips this model. Key components such as subnets, firewalls, load balancers, and VPNs are deployed as services. These services can be defined via code, replicated across regions, and scaled on demand.

Comparison Table

Feature	Traditional Networking	Cloud Networking (Azure)
Infrastructure	Physical devices	Virtualized services
Scalability	Manual, hardware-limited	Elastic, software-defined
Automation	Limited	High (via ARM, Bicep, CLI)
Cost	High CapEx	Pay-as-you-go OpEx
Deployment Speed	Slow	Rapid, template-driven

The Shift to Software-Defined Networking (SDN)

At the heart of cloud networking lies Software-Defined Networking (SDN), which decouples the control plane from the data plane. This separation enables centralized control and dynamic provisioning of networking resources.

In Azure, SDN powers services like Virtual Networks, Network Security Groups (NSGs), Azure Firewall, and Application Gateway. You can define complex topologies and rulesets using ARM templates or tools like Bicep, PowerShell, or the Azure CLI.

Example using Azure CLI to create a VNet:

```
az network vnet create \
  --name MyVNet \
  --resource-group MyResourceGroup \
  --location eastus \
  --address-prefix 10.0.0.0/16 \
  --subnet-name MySubnet \
  --subnet-prefix 10.0.1.0/24
```

This command alone provisions an isolated, cloud-native network environment ready for compute, storage, and application workloads.

Multi-Tenancy and Isolation

One of the pillars of cloud networking is **multi-tenancy**—the ability to host multiple customers (tenants) on the same infrastructure while keeping their resources and traffic isolated. Azure accomplishes this through network segmentation at the VNet and subscription levels, with robust access control enforced by Azure Active Directory (AAD) and Role-Based Access Control (RBAC).

Each Azure subscription acts as a boundary for resource management, billing, and network scope. Virtual Networks are isolated unless explicitly peered, ensuring that tenants cannot accidentally or maliciously access each other's data.

Programmability and Infrastructure as Code (IaC)

Cloud networking is inherently programmable. Azure provides several tools to define and manage network infrastructure as code, including:

- **ARM Templates**: JSON-based definitions used for declarative resource provisioning.

- **Bicep**: A more readable DSL for ARM.

- **Terraform**: A popular third-party tool supporting multi-cloud deployments.

- **Azure CLI & PowerShell**: Scriptable tools for imperative workflows.

This paradigm enables repeatable deployments, version control, and alignment with DevOps pipelines. For example, a network architecture defined in a `.bicep` file can be deployed across dev, test, and production environments with confidence.

Zero Trust Networking

A modern cloud networking model embraces **Zero Trust** principles—never trust, always verify. Azure integrates Zero Trust by enforcing identity validation, encryption, micro-segmentation, and continuous monitoring.

Consider these components:

- **NSGs and ASGs**: Control traffic at subnet or NIC level.

- **Azure Firewall**: Stateful inspection and threat intelligence.

- **Private Link**: Limits exposure to public internet.

A Zero Trust model in Azure involves:

1. Strong authentication via Azure AD and Multi-Factor Authentication (MFA).

2. Least-privilege access using NSGs and RBAC.

3. Logging and monitoring with Azure Monitor and Sentinel.

Networking as a Platform

Unlike traditional environments, Azure treats networking as a **platform service**, tightly integrated with identity, compute, storage, and PaaS components. You no longer manage networking in isolation; instead, it becomes a programmable, observable, and composable part of your overall architecture.

Azure networking supports:

- **Dynamic DNS updates**

- **Auto-scaling with Application Gateway**

- **Custom routing with User Defined Routes (UDRs)**

- **End-to-end encryption using TLS and IPsec**

This integration fosters a more agile, secure, and resilient approach to infrastructure design.

Cloud-Native Challenges and Considerations

While Azure networking offers powerful capabilities, it's not without complexity. Consider the following challenges:

- **Subnet exhaustion**: Planning IP ranges for future growth.

- **Hybrid integration**: Managing latency and compliance in hybrid scenarios.

- **Shared responsibility model**: Understanding what Azure secures vs. what you must secure.

It's crucial to design with automation, scalability, and governance in mind. For example, tagging and naming conventions should be established early to aid cost tracking and operational clarity.

Conclusion

Understanding cloud networking paradigms is the first step toward building secure, scalable, and manageable infrastructure in Azure. By leveraging virtual networks, software-defined controls, and infrastructure-as-code tools, you can create environments that are not only technically sound but also aligned with modern security and DevOps practices.

The rest of this book will guide you through this journey—deep diving into specific services, configurations, and real-world patterns that make Azure networking a cornerstone of enterprise cloud success.

Why Azure for Secure Network Architecture

As organizations migrate to the cloud or adopt hybrid environments, ensuring secure, scalable, and manageable network architecture becomes a critical part of IT strategy. Microsoft Azure provides a robust, integrated platform for designing and managing network infrastructure with a strong emphasis on security, compliance, and operational efficiency. This section explores why Azure is uniquely suited for building secure network architectures, highlighting key advantages, services, and methodologies that support modern enterprise needs.

Built-In Security and Compliance

Azure has been architected from the ground up with security as a foundational principle. Microsoft invests over $1 billion annually in cybersecurity and employs more than 3,500 cybersecurity professionals to protect its infrastructure. Azure's security model spans multiple layers: physical, infrastructure, network, application, and data.

Security by Design

Security is embedded at every level of the Azure stack. Key security features include:

- **Isolation by default**: Each Azure subscription is isolated. Virtual Networks (VNets) do not overlap unless peered explicitly.

- **Integrated Role-Based Access Control (RBAC)**: Access to resources can be precisely controlled at various scopes (subscription, resource group, or resource).

- **Just-in-Time (JIT) access**: Limits exposure by granting temporary administrative access to VMs.

- **DDoS protection**: Azure provides built-in basic DDoS protection and optional standard-tier protection to safeguard against volumetric, protocol, and resource layer attacks.

Compliance Certifications

Azure meets a broad set of international and industry-specific compliance standards, including:

- **ISO/IEC** **27001,** **27017,** **and** **27018**

- **SOC** **1,** **2,** **and** **3**

- **GDPR**

- **HIPAA**

- **FedRAMP** **High**

- **UK** **G-Cloud**

These certifications demonstrate Azure's commitment to secure handling of sensitive workloads, particularly important in healthcare, finance, government, and regulated industries.

Azure Networking Services: Security-Centric Design

Azure's networking stack is extensive and offers deep security integration at every layer. Below are some of the primary services and how they contribute to secure architecture.

Virtual Network (VNet)

A VNet is the foundational building block for private networking in Azure. It enables:

- IP address space definition

- Subnetting

- Route control with UDRs (User Defined Routes)

- Network peering

- Isolation from other VNets and subscriptions

VNets are private and non-routable by default, ensuring that only explicitly defined connections (e.g., VPN or ExpressRoute) allow ingress or egress traffic.

Network Security Groups (NSGs)

NSGs function like access control lists (ACLs) for Azure resources. They allow or deny traffic to/from subnets or individual NICs based on defined rules. Example rule to allow HTTP traffic:

```
az network nsg rule create \
  --resource-group MyResourceGroup \
  --nsg-name MyNSG \
  --name Allow-HTTP \
  --protocol Tcp \
  --direction Inbound \
  --priority 100 \
  --source-address-prefixes '*' \
  --source-port-ranges '*' \
  --destination-address-prefixes '*' \
  --destination-port-ranges 80 \
  --access Allow
```

This granular control is essential for implementing micro-segmentation and least privilege principles.

Azure Firewall

Azure Firewall is a cloud-native, stateful firewall as a service with built-in high availability and unrestricted scalability. It supports:

- Application and network rule collections

- Threat intelligence filtering

- FQDN-based filtering

- Logging via Azure Monitor

Unlike NSGs, which are stateless, Azure Firewall offers comprehensive traffic filtering, inspection, and logging for both inbound and outbound traffic.

Application Gateway and WAF

Azure Application Gateway is a layer 7 load balancer that includes Web Application Firewall (WAF) capabilities. It protects web applications against common vulnerabilities such as SQL injection and cross-site scripting (XSS). WAF rules are based on the OWASP Core Rule Set (CRS) and can be customized for specific applications.

This is ideal for public-facing web apps that need TLS termination, session affinity, and advanced routing.

Identity-Driven Security

Azure seamlessly integrates with **Azure Active Directory (AAD)** to ensure that access to network resources is identity-aware. This aligns with Zero Trust principles, enforcing access based on who the user is, their device status, and contextual information.

Examples of identity-based features include:

- **Conditional Access**: Grant/deny access based on location, risk level, or compliance status.

- **Managed Identities**: Allow Azure services to authenticate with each other securely without storing credentials.

- **Integration with Azure Policy**: Ensure only compliant network configurations are allowed.

For instance, you can restrict Virtual Network access so that only users from a specific security group can deploy or modify configurations.

End-to-End Encryption

Encryption is a fundamental requirement for secure networks. Azure ensures data is encrypted:

- **In transit**: Using TLS, IPSec (VPN), and ExpressRoute encryption options.

- **At rest**: With Azure Storage Service Encryption (SSE) and customer-managed keys (CMKs) via Key Vault.

- **Between services**: Using Private Link and service endpoints to avoid internet exposure.

Private Link allows access to Azure PaaS services like Azure SQL or Azure Storage over a private IP, eliminating the need for public endpoints.

Example: Creating a Private Endpoint for Azure SQL

```
az network private-endpoint create \
  --name myPrivateEndpoint \
  --resource-group MyResourceGroup \
  --vnet-name MyVNet \
  --subnet MySubnet \
  --private-connection-resource-id
/subscriptions/.../resourceGroups/.../providers/Microsoft.Sql/server
s/mySqlServer \
  --group-ids sqlServer
```

This ensures that sensitive services stay off the public internet and are accessible only through internal IPs.

Scalable and Resilient Architecture

Secure network architecture also implies high availability and resilience. Azure enables you to build architectures that are fault-tolerant and resistant to both attacks and unplanned outages.

Design elements include:

- **Availability Zones**: Spread resources across physically separate data centers.

- **Load Balancers**: Both L4 (Basic/Standard) and L7 (Application Gateway) options.

- **Traffic Manager**: Geo-distribution and failover routing.

- **Multi-region deployments**: Ensures continuity even if an entire region fails.

Azure's global backbone, which spans hundreds of thousands of miles of fiber, also offers unparalleled performance and resilience, especially when using services like ExpressRoute or Azure Front Door.

Network Monitoring and Threat Detection

Monitoring is integral to security. Azure provides several tools that deliver visibility into your network:

- **Network Watcher**: Packet capture, connection monitoring, and topology views.

- **Azure Monitor and Log Analytics**: Aggregates and queries logs from NSGs, firewalls, and other resources.

- **Microsoft Defender for Cloud**: Assesses security posture and provides actionable insights.

- **Sentinel**: Azure-native SIEM solution for detecting and responding to threats.

Example: Enabling diagnostics for a network interface

```
az network nic show \
  --resource-group MyResourceGroup \
  --name MyNIC \
  --query "diagnosticSettings"
```

These tools help you identify misconfigurations, detect intrusions, and maintain a strong security posture across your network environment.

Governance and Policy Enforcement

Secure architectures are also governed architectures. Azure Policy and Azure Blueprints let you enforce compliance across your network resources automatically.

Examples include:

- Ensuring all VNets have NSGs attached.

- Blocking public IP creation unless explicitly required.

- Mandating diagnostic logging for firewalls and gateways.

Azure Policy example to deny creation of public IPs:

```
{
  "if": {
    "field": "type",
    "equals": "Microsoft.Network/publicIPAddresses"
  },
  "then": {
    "effect": "deny"
  }
}
```

This level of control helps maintain consistency and compliance without manual auditing.

Cost Efficiency and Operational Simplicity

Azure's pay-as-you-go pricing and automation capabilities make it easier to manage and secure networks without the capital expense and operational complexity of traditional setups.

Features contributing to cost-effective security:

- **Scaling   down   or   automating   idle   infrastructure**

- **Using   Azure   Reservations   for   long-term   workloads**

- **Integrated   cost   analysis   tools**

These considerations help ensure that securing your network doesn't mean overextending your budget.

Conclusion

Azure stands out as a comprehensive platform for building secure, scalable, and compliant network architectures. With deep integration between networking, identity, compute, and security services, Azure enables organizations to implement Zero Trust models, enforce governance, and monitor networks proactively.

Whether you're building a simple VNet for a development environment or architecting a globally distributed, highly secure infrastructure for regulated industries, Azure provides the tools, services, and frameworks to support you. Understanding why Azure is a preferred choice for secure network architecture lays the groundwork for deploying robust, production-ready environments throughout your cloud journey.

Core Azure Networking Services Overview

To design, implement, and maintain modern network architectures in Microsoft Azure, it's crucial to understand the core networking services the platform provides. These services form the building blocks for secure connectivity, traffic routing, load distribution, remote access, and hybrid integration. This section dives deep into the most essential Azure networking services, explaining their roles, configuration principles, and integration potential within broader cloud or hybrid architectures.

Virtual Network (VNet)

The Azure Virtual Network (VNet) is the foundational element of networking in Azure. It provides an isolated, logical network segment in which you can deploy and connect Azure resources such as virtual machines (VMs), containers, and platform services.

Key characteristics of VNets include:

- **Customizable   IP   address   spaces**   using   CIDR   blocks.

- **Subnetting**   for   traffic   segmentation.

- **Isolation   by   default**,   with   optional   peering   for   controlled   access.

- **Security   integration**   via   NSGs,   ASGs,   and   firewalls.

Creating a VNet with a subnet using Azure CLI:

```
az network vnet create \
  --resource-group MyResourceGroup \
  --name MyVNet \
  --address-prefix 10.0.0.0/16 \
  --subnet-name MySubnet \
  --subnet-prefix 10.0.1.0/24
```

VNets can span availability zones, support service endpoints for direct access to Azure services, and connect across regions using Global VNet Peering.

Subnets and Address Spaces

Within a VNet, subnets divide the address space into manageable sections. This segmentation allows:

- Isolation   of   workloads   (e.g.,   front-end,   back-end,   database).

- Application   of   security   policies   at   the   subnet   level.

- Routing   customization   using   route   tables   and   BGP.

You can associate different NSGs and route tables with each subnet, providing flexible control over traffic behavior.

Example: Adding a new subnet

```
az network vnet subnet create \
  --address-prefixes 10.0.2.0/24 \
  --name BackendSubnet \
  --resource-group MyResourceGroup \
  --vnet-name MyVNet
```

Planning subnet address spaces to avoid overlap is vital when designing hybrid or multi-region environments.

Network Security Groups (NSGs)

NSGs act as virtual firewalls, controlling inbound and outbound traffic to network interfaces, subnets, and VMs. Each NSG contains rules that define allowed or denied traffic.

Typical use cases include:

- Allowing HTTP/HTTPS to web servers.

- Restricting database access to a specific subnet.

- Blocking all internet access from a sensitive subnet.

An NSG rule example:

```
az network nsg rule create \
  --resource-group MyResourceGroup \
  --nsg-name WebNSG \
  --name AllowWeb \
  --protocol Tcp \
  --direction Inbound \
  --priority 100 \
  --source-address-prefix Internet \
  --source-port-range "*" \
  --destination-address-prefix "*" \
  --destination-port-range 80 443 \
  --access Allow
```

NSGs are critical for enforcing least-privilege access across environments and are deeply integrated into Azure monitoring tools for audit and diagnostics.

Application Security Groups (ASGs)

ASGs simplify NSG rule management by allowing you to group resources logically. Instead of targeting specific IPs or NICs, you can apply rules to an ASG.

Benefits:

- Reduced complexity in environments with dynamic IPs.

- Centralized grouping for tiered applications.

- Enhanced scalability in large deployments.

Example:

- Define a `WebASG` for all front-end VMs.

- Create an NSG rule allowing traffic from `WebASG` to `AppASG` on port 443.

This abstraction is extremely useful in enterprise-scale deployments where manual IP-based rules are error-prone.

Azure Load Balancer

The Azure Load Balancer operates at Layer 4 (TCP/UDP) and offers both public and internal load balancing. It's used to distribute incoming network traffic across multiple VMs, enhancing fault tolerance and scalability.

Key features:

- **Inbound NAT rules** for remote VM access.

- **Outbound rules** to provide internet access.

- **Health probes** to ensure traffic is only sent to healthy backends.

- **Integration with VM scale sets** for auto-scaling apps.

Example: Creating a Basic Load Balancer

```
az network lb create \
  --resource-group MyResourceGroup \
  --name MyLoadBalancer \
  --sku Basic \
  --frontend-ip-name MyFrontEnd \
  --backend-pool-name MyBackEndPool
```

While suitable for simple scenarios, consider using the Standard SKU for production due to its broader capabilities, availability zones support, and enhanced metrics.

Application Gateway and Web Application Firewall (WAF)

Azure Application Gateway is a Layer 7 (HTTP/HTTPS) load balancer capable of intelligent routing, SSL termination, and application firewalling. It supports:

- URL-based routing

- Session affinity

- SSL offloading

- Web Application Firewall (WAF) based on OWASP rules

This service is ideal for enterprise-grade web applications with strict security requirements.

WAF protects against common threats like:

- SQL injection

- Cross-site scripting (XSS)

- HTTP protocol violations

Example: Enabling WAF with Application Gateway

```
az network application-gateway waf-config set \
  --enabled true \
  --gateway-name MyAppGateway \
  --resource-group MyResourceGroup \
  --firewall-mode Prevention
```

App Gateway is tightly integrated with Azure Kubernetes Service (AKS), making it an excellent choice for microservices-based applications.

Azure DNS and Private DNS Zones

Azure DNS enables you to host your domains on Azure infrastructure, providing ultra-low-latency name resolution with global availability.

Benefits include:

- Use of Azure's globally distributed name servers.

- Integration with ARM for IaC deployments.

- DNS record management via CLI, REST API, or Portal.

Private DNS zones allow resolution of custom domain names within a VNet without exposing them to the public internet. They are essential in microservice or hybrid architectures.

Example: Creating a private DNS zone

```
az network private-dns zone create \
  --resource-group MyResourceGroup \
  --name contoso.internal
```

DNS in Azure supports split-horizon scenarios where internal and external names resolve differently, providing flexibility in hybrid use cases.

Azure Firewall

Azure Firewall is a stateful firewall as a service, allowing central governance of all outbound and inbound traffic across VNets and regions.

Features include:

- **Threat intelligence** integration for known malicious IPs/domains.

- **Application rules** with FQDN filtering.

- **Network rules** for protocol and port-based control.

- **Logging and diagnostics** through Azure Monitor and Log Analytics.

Example: Creating an Azure Firewall

```
az network firewall create \
  --name MyFirewall \
  --resource-group MyResourceGroup \
  --location eastus
```

It's often used in hub-and-spoke architectures to centralize traffic inspection and egress control.

VPN Gateway

Azure VPN Gateway enables secure, cross-premises connectivity between your on-premises networks and Azure VNets over IPsec/IKE VPN tunnels.

Options:

- **Site-to-Site VPN** for permanent, encrypted tunnel-based connectivity.

- **Point-to-Site VPN** for remote user access.

- **VNet-to-VNet VPN** for connecting Azure regions or subscriptions.

Example: Creating a VPN gateway

```
az network vpn-gateway create \
  --name MyVpnGateway \
  --public-ip-address MyPublicIP \
  --resource-group MyResourceGroup \
  --vnet MyVNet \
  --gateway-type Vpn \
  --vpn-type RouteBased
```

This is commonly used in hybrid cloud designs where ExpressRoute is unavailable or overkill.

ExpressRoute

For high-performance, dedicated connectivity, Azure ExpressRoute offers private connections between on-premises networks and Azure datacenters. It bypasses the public internet entirely, resulting in:

- Lower latency

- Increased privacy

- SLA-backed reliability

Use cases:

- Mission-critical financial or healthcare systems.

- Data sovereignty and compliance requirements.

- High-throughput data transfer scenarios.

ExpressRoute circuits support peering with Microsoft services, private VNets, and Azure public endpoints.

Azure Bastion

Azure Bastion provides secure and seamless RDP/SSH access to Azure VMs directly from the portal without exposing public IPs. It's ideal for administrators who need to manage VMs securely over the internet without configuring jump boxes or VPNs.

Example: Creating a Bastion host

```
az network bastion create \
  --name MyBastion \
  --resource-group MyResourceGroup \
  --vnet-name MyVNet \
  --public-ip-address MyPublicIP \
  --location eastus
```

This service supports browser-based session access with full security auditing, making it a best practice for operational security.

Summary

Azure provides a comprehensive suite of core networking services that empower organizations to build secure, scalable, and flexible cloud networks. These services—ranging from VNets and NSGs to load balancers, firewalls, and ExpressRoute—form a cohesive ecosystem capable of supporting any cloud networking need.

Each service integrates tightly with Azure identity, security, and governance frameworks, allowing teams to enforce policies, monitor usage, and automate deployments confidently. Whether you're creating a simple test environment or designing a global hybrid architecture, mastering these core services is essential to achieving operational success in Azure.

Setting Up Your Azure Environment

Before deploying any network resources or configuring secure architectures in Azure, it's essential to understand how to properly set up your Azure environment. This includes configuring subscriptions, organizing resources through logical groupings, understanding access control, setting up automation tools, and preparing your environment for infrastructure-as-code (IaC) deployments. A well-structured environment ensures scalability, maintainability, cost control, and security.

This section will walk you through the key steps and best practices to get your Azure environment ready for real-world networking deployments.

Azure Account and Subscription Hierarchy

To begin working with Azure, you need a Microsoft account or an Azure Active Directory (AAD) tenant. When you sign up for Azure, you're assigned a default **subscription**, which acts as a container for all your Azure resources.

Azure subscription hierarchy:

- **Account**: Your billing entity.
- **Tenant (Directory)**: Represents the AAD identity environment.

- **Subscription**: Logical container for resources; tied to billing.

- **Resource Groups**: Logical groupings of resources within a subscription.

It's best practice to use **multiple subscriptions** when managing different environments such as development, staging, and production, especially in enterprise scenarios. This allows for isolation, separate billing, and independent access control.

You can create new subscriptions through the Azure Portal or via CLI:

```
az account subscription create --offer-type MS-AZR-0017P --display-name "Prod Subscription"
```

Use `az account set` to switch between subscriptions:

```
az account set --subscription "Prod Subscription"
```

Organizing with Resource Groups

Resource Groups are a critical organizational unit in Azure. They allow you to group resources that share a common lifecycle, such as a set of VMs, VNets, and load balancers supporting an application.

Advantages:

- Simplified permission management.

- Easier automation.

- Resource scoping for cost and policy control.

- Supports bulk operations like deletion or tagging.

Creating a resource group:

```
az group create \
  --name NetworkRG \
  --location eastus
```

Keep related resources in the same group, but don't overload a single group with unrelated services. It's also wise to follow a naming convention for consistency across the organization (e.g., `rg-dev-network`, `rg-prod-security`).

Identity and Access Management (IAM)

Access to your Azure environment is controlled by Azure Active Directory (AAD) using Role-Based Access Control (RBAC). RBAC assigns roles to users, groups, or service principals at different scopes: subscription, resource group, or individual resource.

Common roles include:

- **Owner**: Full access including assigning roles.

- **Contributor**: Can manage resources but not assign access.

- **Reader**: View-only access.

Example: Assigning a Contributor role to a user for a resource group

```
az role assignment create \
  --assignee john@contoso.com \
  --role Contributor \
  --resource-group NetworkRG
```

You can create custom roles for more fine-grained control or use **Management Groups** to apply policies across multiple subscriptions.

Naming Conventions and Tagging

Implementing a consistent naming convention is foundational to scalable and maintainable infrastructure. A common pattern includes the environment, region, resource type, and identifier:

```
vnet-prod-eastus-core
nsg-dev-westus-web
vm-stg-eastus-db01
```

Azure supports **tags** as key-value pairs applied to resources and resource groups for categorization and cost analysis:

```
az tag create --name "Environment" --value "Production"
az resource tag --resource-id
/subscriptions/.../resourceGroups/NetworkRG/providers/Microsoft.Netw
ork/virtualNetworks/vnet-prod-eastus-core --tags
Environment=Production Department=IT
```

Tags are essential for enforcing governance, cost tracking, and operational management via Azure Policy and Cost Management.

Azure CLI and PowerShell Setup

For automation and repeatable deployments, you'll want to configure command-line tools. Azure supports:

- **Azure**   **CLI**   (cross-platform)

- **Azure**   **PowerShell**   (Windows-focused)

- **Azure**   **Cloud**   **Shell**   (browser-based,   preconfigured)

To install Azure CLI:

```
curl -sL https://aka.ms/InstallAzureCLIDeb | sudo bash
az login
```

Once authenticated, you can script out deployments, query resources, and manage infrastructure.

Example: List all VNets in a subscription

```
az network vnet list --output table
```

This command-line interface allows you to build CI/CD pipelines and automate environment builds.

Infrastructure as Code (IaC) Preparation

Modern Azure environments are typically defined using Infrastructure as Code. Azure supports several IaC options:

- **ARM**   **Templates**:   Native   JSON-based   templates.

- **Bicep**:   A   domain-specific   language   (DSL)   that   simplifies   ARM.

- **Terraform**: A multi-cloud tool popular for complex infrastructure definitions.

You should prepare your environment to support versioned, repeatable deployments of network components.

Example Bicep file to create a Virtual Network:

```
resource vnet 'Microsoft.Network/virtualNetworks@2021-02-01' = {
  name: 'vnet-dev-eastus'
  location: 'eastus'
  properties: {
    addressSpace: {
      addressPrefixes: [
        '10.0.0.0/16'
      ]
    }
    subnets: [
      {
        name: 'subnet1'
        properties: {
          addressPrefix: '10.0.1.0/24'
        }
      }
    ]
  }
}
```

To deploy this using Azure CLI:

```
az deployment group create \
  --resource-group NetworkRG \
  --template-file vnet.bicep
```

This level of automation ensures consistency across environments and supports agile infrastructure management.

Policy, Compliance, and Governance

To maintain a secure and compliant environment, use **Azure Policy** to enforce standards. For instance, you can require that all network resources be deployed in approved regions, have diagnostic logging enabled, or deny public IPs.

Creating a policy definition to restrict regions:

```
{
  "if": {
    "not": {
      "field": "location",
      "in": ["eastus", "westus2"]
```

```
    }
  },
  "then": {
    "effect": "deny"
  }
}
```

Apply this policy across your subscription to ensure consistent compliance with organizational standards.

Governance tools include:

- **Azure Blueprints**: Predefined environment templates.

- **Management Groups**: Apply governance across subscriptions.

- **Resource Locks**: Prevent accidental deletion.

Example: Locking a resource group

```
az lock create \
  --name ProtectNetworkRG \
  --resource-group NetworkRG \
  --lock-type CanNotDelete
```

Logging, Monitoring, and Alerts

Before deploying resources, configure monitoring services like:

- **Azure**   **Monitor**

- **Log**   **Analytics**

- **Network**   **Watcher**

- **Activity**   **Logs**

Enable diagnostics for all critical resources such as firewalls, load balancers, and VNets.

Example: Enabling diagnostics on a VNet

```
az monitor diagnostic-settings create \
  --name VNetDiagnostics \
```

```
  --resource
/subscriptions/.../resourceGroups/NetworkRG/providers/Microsoft.Netw
ork/virtualNetworks/vnet-dev-eastus \
  --workspace
/subscriptions/.../resourceGroups/MonitoringRG/providers/Microsoft.O
perationalInsights/workspaces/loganalyticsworkspace \
  --logs '[{"category":"VMProtectionAlerts","enabled":true}]'
```

Set up alerts for unusual activity such as:

- Excessive   NSG   rule   changes

- Unusual   outbound   traffic   patterns

- New   public   IP   allocations

These practices help maintain network visibility and enable quick response to security or performance issues.

Creating a Baseline Network Environment

Let's walk through creating a basic Azure network environment with key elements:

1. **Resource**   **Group**:   Logical   container

2. **VNet**:   Private   network   space

3. **Subnet**:   Segmentation

4. **NSG**:   Traffic   control

5. **VM**:   Compute   resource

```
az group create --name DevRG --location eastus

az network vnet create \
  --resource-group DevRG \
  --name DevVNet \
  --address-prefix 10.1.0.0/16 \
  --subnet-name WebSubnet \
  --subnet-prefix 10.1.1.0/24

az network nsg create --resource-group DevRG --name WebNSG
```

```
az network nsg rule create \
  --resource-group DevRG \
  --nsg-name WebNSG \
  --name AllowHTTP \
  --protocol Tcp \
  --direction Inbound \
  --priority 100 \
  --source-address-prefix '*' \
  --destination-port-range 80 \
  --access Allow

az vm create \
  --resource-group DevRG \
  --name WebVM \
  --image UbuntuLTS \
  --vnet-name DevVNet \
  --subnet WebSubnet \
  --nsg WebNSG \
  --admin-username azureuser \
  --generate-ssh-keys
```

This creates a secure, accessible development environment that follows basic best practices and can be extended for more advanced scenarios.

Conclusion

Setting up your Azure environment correctly is a crucial step in preparing for secure and scalable networking deployments. By understanding subscription management, enforcing governance, using automation tools, applying security policies, and structuring your environment with best practices, you lay a strong foundation for future growth and operational excellence.

As we move into the next chapters, these fundamentals will be essential as we explore more advanced configurations like virtual network peering, hybrid connectivity, and network security architectures. A robust environment setup not only simplifies operations but also enhances security, efficiency, and agility across the board.

Chapter 2: Foundations of Azure Virtual Networks

Creating and Configuring VNets

Creating and configuring Virtual Networks (VNets) is one of the most foundational tasks in any Azure deployment. VNets act as isolated networks within Azure, much like traditional on-premises networks, but with the added flexibility and scalability that cloud infrastructure brings. This section will guide you through the principles of planning, creating, and configuring VNets, along with best practices to ensure a secure and efficient design.

Understanding Virtual Networks

A Virtual Network is a logically isolated section of the Azure cloud dedicated to your subscription. It allows Azure resources to securely communicate with each other, the internet, and on-premises networks.

Each VNet spans a single Azure region but can connect across regions using **Global VNet Peering**. VNets can host resources such as:

- Virtual   machines

- App   services   with   regional   VNet   integration

- Azure   Kubernetes   Service   nodes

- Azure   Bastion,   gateways,   and   firewalls

VNets are defined by their IP address space using CIDR notation (e.g., `10.0.0.0/16`) and contain subnets, which further divide this address space for segmentation and control.

Planning VNet Architecture

Before creating a VNet, consider the following:

- **IP addressing strategy**: Choose a non-overlapping IP range that avoids conflicts with on-prem   or   future   peered   networks.

- **Region selection**: Determine which Azure region the VNet will reside in. This affects latency,   availability   zones,   and   regulatory   compliance.

- **Subnet planning**: Subnet your network according to tiers (web, application, database),   workloads,   or   security   zones.

- **Naming conventions**: Establish consistent naming for traceability (e.g., `vnet-prod-eastus-core`).

- **Future scaling**: Plan for growth by reserving space for future subnets and services.

Use a tool like an IP planning spreadsheet or diagramming software to visualize your architecture.

Creating a VNet Using the Azure Portal

To create a VNet via the Azure Portal:

1. Navigate to **Virtual Networks**.

2. Click **Create** > **Virtual Network**.

3. Select a subscription and resource group.

4. Name your VNet (e.g., `vnet-dev-eastus`).

5. Choose a region.

6. Define the IP address space (e.g., `10.1.0.0/16`).

7. Add subnets (e.g., `10.1.1.0/24` for web, `10.1.2.0/24` for app).

8. Review and create.

This interactive approach is suitable for initial testing or smaller environments.

Creating a VNet Using Azure CLI

For infrastructure automation or scripting, Azure CLI offers a more repeatable method:

```
az network vnet create \
  --resource-group DevRG \
  --name vnet-dev-eastus \
  --address-prefix 10.1.0.0/16 \
  --subnet-name WebSubnet \
  --subnet-prefix 10.1.1.0/24 \
  --location eastus
```

This creates a VNet and a single subnet named `WebSubnet`. You can add more subnets later using:

```
az network vnet subnet create \
  --address-prefix 10.1.2.0/24 \
  --name AppSubnet \
  --resource-group DevRG \
  --vnet-name vnet-dev-eastus
```

Configuring DNS and Name Resolution

By default, Azure provides name resolution for resources within a VNet. However, you can configure:

- **Custom DNS servers**: Useful for hybrid or private DNS management.

- **Azure DNS Private Zones**: Internal DNS resolution without external exposure.

To set a custom DNS server for a VNet:

```
az network vnet update \
  --name vnet-dev-eastus \
  --resource-group DevRG \
  --dns-servers 10.0.0.4 10.0.0.5
```

Use this when integrating with on-premises DNS infrastructure or enforcing internal naming standards.

Associating Network Security Groups (NSGs)

NSGs control traffic to and from resources in a VNet. You can associate NSGs with:

- Subnets   (applies   to   all   NICs   within)

- Network   Interfaces   (granular   control)

To associate an NSG to a subnet:

```
az network vnet subnet update \
  --vnet-name vnet-dev-eastus \
  --name WebSubnet \
  --resource-group DevRG \
  --network-security-group WebNSG
```

This is a crucial step in implementing Zero Trust and network segmentation policies.

Integrating Service Endpoints

Azure service endpoints extend VNet private address spaces to Azure services, enabling secure connections without a public IP. Supported services include:

- Azure   Storage

- Azure   SQL   Database

- Key   Vault

- Cosmos   DB

Enable a service endpoint on a subnet:

```
az network vnet subnet update \
  --name WebSubnet \
  --resource-group DevRG \
  --vnet-name vnet-dev-eastus \
  --service-endpoints Microsoft.Storage
```

After enabling, configure the storage account to accept traffic **only** from your VNet for maximum security.

Enabling Private Endpoints

Private Endpoints provide private IP addresses for Azure PaaS resources within your VNet. Unlike service endpoints, they bring the service **into** your VNet via a NIC.

Use this for:

- Regulatory   isolation

- Auditing   traffic   via   NSGs   and   route   tables

- Eliminating   outbound   traffic   to   public   IPs

Example:

```
az network private-endpoint create \
  --name storage-pe \
  --resource-group DevRG \
  --vnet-name vnet-dev-eastus \
  --subnet WebSubnet \
```

```
  --private-connection-resource-id
/subscriptions/.../resourceGroups/.../providers/Microsoft.Storage/st
orageAccounts/mystorageaccount \
  --group-ids blob
```

Private Endpoints are a best practice for high-security or compliance-sensitive environments.

VNet Peering Configuration

To allow communication between two VNets in the same or different regions, use VNet Peering. Peered VNets behave like a single network, with low latency and high throughput.

Example: Peer two VNets

```
az network vnet peering create \
  --name LinkToProd \
  --resource-group DevRG \
  --vnet-name vnet-dev-eastus \
  --remote-vnet
/subscriptions/.../resourceGroups/ProdRG/providers/Microsoft.Network
/virtualNetworks/vnet-prod-eastus \
  --allow-vnet-access
```

Ensure that IP address ranges do not overlap, and configure corresponding peering from the other VNet for bi-directional communication.

User Defined Routes (UDRs)

UDRs allow you to override Azure's default routing behavior. Use cases include:

- Sending traffic through a firewall
- Routing traffic to a virtual appliance (NVA)
- Forcing internet traffic through an on-premises VPN

Create a route table and apply it to a subnet:

```
az network route-table create \
  --name MyRouteTable \
  --resource-group DevRG \
  --location eastus
```

```
az network route-table route create \
  --resource-group DevRG \
  --route-table-name MyRouteTable \
  --name RouteToFirewall \
  --address-prefix 0.0.0.0/0 \
  --next-hop-type VirtualAppliance \
  --next-hop-ip-address 10.1.3.4

az network vnet subnet update \
  --vnet-name vnet-dev-eastus \
  --name AppSubnet \
  --resource-group DevRG \
  --route-table MyRouteTable
```

Always test route behavior after applying UDRs to avoid breaking access to Azure services.

Logging and Monitoring Your VNet

Azure supports deep monitoring of VNet resources using:

- **Network Watcher**: Packet capture, NSG flow logs, topology views.

- **Azure Monitor**: Resource-level metrics and alerts.

- **Log Analytics**: Queryable logs for diagnostics.

Enable NSG flow logs:

```
az network watcher flow-log configure \
  --resource-group DevRG \
  --nsg WebNSG \
  --enabled true \
  --retention 30 \
  --storage-account mystorageacct \
  --traffic-analytics true \
  --workspace
/subscriptions/.../resourceGroups/MonitoringRG/providers/Microsoft.O
perationalInsights/workspaces/loganalytics
```

These insights are vital for performance troubleshooting and security auditing.

Automation with Infrastructure as Code (IaC)

To ensure consistency across environments, define VNets using ARM, Bicep, or Terraform.

Example Bicep template:

```
resource vnet 'Microsoft.Network/virtualNetworks@2021-02-01' = {
  name: 'vnet-dev-eastus'
  location: 'eastus'
  properties: {
    addressSpace: {
      addressPrefixes: [
        '10.1.0.0/16'
      ]
    }
    subnets: [
      {
        name: 'WebSubnet'
        properties: {
          addressPrefix: '10.1.1.0/24'
        }
      }
    ]
  }
}
```

Deploy using Azure CLI:

```
az deployment group create \
  --resource-group DevRG \
  --template-file vnet.bicep
```

IaC ensures repeatability, reduces manual errors, and aligns with DevOps practices.

Summary

Creating and configuring VNets in Azure is the cornerstone of any secure and scalable cloud environment. From planning IP address spaces and subnets to applying NSGs, integrating service endpoints, enabling private connectivity, and implementing peering or custom routes, every decision impacts the architecture's performance, security, and manageability.

By leveraging Azure's CLI tools, automation capabilities, and monitoring systems, you can build reliable networks that adapt to both current workloads and future demands. With your foundational VNet in place, you're now ready to dive into deeper networking topics like subnetting strategies, IP management, and interconnectivity, which will be covered in the following sections.

Subnetting Strategies and Use Cases

Subnetting in Azure Virtual Networks (VNets) is a powerful tool that enables you to segment networks, enforce security policies, manage workloads efficiently, and support scaling strategies. A well-planned subnetting strategy lays the foundation for secure, resilient, and scalable network design in the cloud. In this section, we will explore how subnetting works in Azure, best practices for subnet design, and real-world use cases, while diving deep into the architectural reasoning behind subnetting decisions.

What Is Subnetting?

Subnetting is the process of dividing a large IP address space into smaller, more manageable blocks called subnets. Each subnet is a logically distinct segment within the VNet and is associated with a specific IP range defined using Classless Inter-Domain Routing (CIDR) notation.

In Azure, every subnet:

- Must reside within a single VNet.

- Must be associated with a non-overlapping address prefix.

- Cannot span across regions or VNets.

- Can host a mix of resource types (VMs, services, containers).

- Can be associated with NSGs, route tables, and service endpoints.

Example of a VNet with subnetting:

- VNet address space: `10.0.0.0/16`

  - Subnet A: `10.0.1.0/24` (Web tier)

  - Subnet B: `10.0.2.0/24` (Application tier)

  - Subnet C: `10.0.3.0/24` (Database tier)

Each subnet isolates workloads while allowing fine-grained control over access, monitoring, and scaling.

Subnet Planning Considerations

Before creating subnets, carefully plan for:

- **Workload separation**: Organize resources by role (e.g., web, app, db).

- **Security zoning**: Apply different NSGs or firewalls per subnet.

- **Service integration**: Consider where service endpoints or private links will reside.

- **Growth and future-proofing**: Reserve address space for future expansion.

- **Compliance and policy enforcement**: Enforce policies based on subnet scope.

Subnet IP ranges should never overlap and should ideally align with IP conventions used in your organization.

Use a subnet calculator or spreadsheet to plan address space allocation.

CIDR Blocks and Subnet Sizes

CIDR notation is used to define IP ranges. Azure supports from /8 to /29, allowing a range of addressable hosts. However, Azure reserves 5 IPs per subnet:

- First: Network address

- Second to fourth: Reserved by Azure

- Last: Broadcast address

Therefore, in a /24 subnet (256 IPs), only 251 are usable.

Common subnet sizes:

CIDR	Total IPs	Usable IPs	Use Case
/29	8	3	Point-to-site VPN
/28	16	11	Small test workloads
/24	256	251	Web/App tiers
/22	1024	1019	AKS or large services

Be cautious: once a subnet is created, its size cannot be changed. Always leave room for scaling.

Creating Subnets with Azure CLI

You can create subnets within a VNet using the CLI:

```
az network vnet subnet create \
  --resource-group NetworkRG \
  --vnet-name CorpVNet \
  --name WebSubnet \
  --address-prefix 10.0.1.0/24
```

Add multiple subnets with different purposes:

```
az network vnet subnet create \
  --resource-group NetworkRG \
  --vnet-name CorpVNet \
  --name AppSubnet \
  --address-prefix 10.0.2.0/24

az network vnet subnet create \
  --resource-group NetworkRG \
  --vnet-name CorpVNet \
  --name DBSubnet \
  --address-prefix 10.0.3.0/24
```

This segmentation allows isolation and targeted policies.

Subnetting Patterns and Design Models

Tiered Application Model

A three-tier architecture (web, app, database) is a common model. Each tier resides in its own subnet:

- WebSubnet: Exposed to internet via load balancer or Application Gateway.

- AppSubnet: Receives traffic only from WebSubnet.

- DBSubnet: Access limited to AppSubnet only.

Use NSGs and UDRs to enforce inter-subnet policies:

- WebSubnet NSG allows inbound HTTP/HTTPS.

- AppSubnet NSG only allows traffic from WebSubnet.

- DBSubnet NSG blocks all except AppSubnet on port 1433 (SQL).

This segmentation aligns with Zero Trust principles and supports auditability.

Role-Based Subnetting

Instead of tiering by application layers, segment subnets by functional roles:

- `subnet-aks`: Azure Kubernetes Service nodes

- `subnet-bastion`: Secure jump box access

- `subnet-vpn`: VPN Gateway

- `subnet-firewall`: Azure Firewall or NVA

This model simplifies governance and helps manage access at a broader functional level.

Environment-Based Subnetting

Another approach is to segment based on the environment lifecycle:

- `subnet-dev`: Non-production workloads

- `subnet-test`: QA environments

- `subnet-prod`: Production workloads

This makes it easier to apply policies like logging, diagnostics, and tagging based on environment.

Integrating Subnets with NSGs

Once subnets are created, associate NSGs to control traffic:

```
az network nsg create \
  --name WebNSG \
  --resource-group NetworkRG

az network vnet subnet update \
```

```
--vnet-name CorpVNet \
--name WebSubnet \
--resource-group NetworkRG \
--network-security-group WebNSG
```

Use inbound and outbound rules to control access:

```
az network nsg rule create \
  --resource-group NetworkRG \
  --nsg-name WebNSG \
  --name AllowHTTP \
  --protocol Tcp \
  --direction Inbound \
  --priority 100 \
  --source-address-prefix '*' \
  --destination-port-range 80 \
  --access Allow
```

NSGs at the subnet level enforce uniform access control for all NICs within that subnet.

Route Tables for Subnet Traffic Control

User Defined Routes (UDRs) allow you to override Azure's default routing:

- Force traffic through an NVA (e.g., Palo Alto, FortiGate).

- Send internet-bound traffic to on-prem via VPN.

- Create transitive routing between peered VNets.

Example: Direct all subnet traffic to a firewall appliance:

```
az network route-table create \
  --name WebRouteTable \
  --resource-group NetworkRG

az network route-table route create \
  --name DefaultRoute \
  --resource-group NetworkRG \
  --route-table-name WebRouteTable \
  --address-prefix 0.0.0.0/0 \
  --next-hop-type VirtualAppliance \
```

```
  --next-hop-ip-address 10.0.4.4

az network vnet subnet update \
  --vnet-name CorpVNet \
  --name WebSubnet \
  --resource-group NetworkRG \
  --route-table WebRouteTable
```

This ensures all outbound traffic from WebSubnet is inspected.

Private Endpoints and Subnet Isolation

Private Endpoints require careful subnet planning. They inject a NIC into the subnet, consuming an IP and allowing secure access to PaaS services over private IPs.

Design considerations:

- Avoid overlapping subnets with other services.

- Ensure sufficient IP availability for endpoint scaling.

- Apply restrictive NSGs to prevent lateral movement.

Example: Deploying a Private Endpoint into a secure subnet:

```
az network private-endpoint create \
  --name kv-pe \
  --resource-group SecureRG \
  --vnet-name CorpVNet \
  --subnet PrivateEndpointSubnet \
  --private-connection-resource-id
/subscriptions/.../resourceGroups/.../providers/Microsoft.KeyVault/v
aults/myKeyVault \
  --group-ids vault
```

Private Endpoint Subnets should have NSGs that only allow specific source IPs or services.

Subnet Design in Hub-and-Spoke Architectures

In large enterprises, hub-and-spoke models are used for centralizing shared services:

- **Hub VNet**: Hosts firewall, VPN, and shared DNS.

- **Spoke VNets**: Host workloads, segmented by business unit or app.

Within each VNet, subnets follow specific roles:

- Hub:

    o `subnet-firewall`

    o `subnet-gateway`

- Spoke:

    o `subnet-web`

    o `subnet-app`

    o `subnet-db`

Using VNet peering and subnet-level control, traffic is centralized through the hub, ensuring consistent security inspection.

This approach supports:

- Centralized NSG and route table management.
- Simplified auditing and logging.
- Policy enforcement via Azure Firewall Manager.

Monitoring and Subnet Diagnostics

Subnet-level diagnostics include:

- **NSG Flow Logs**: View traffic patterns and rule enforcement.
- **Connection Monitor**: Check VM-to-VM/subnet connectivity.
- **Topology Viewer**: Visualize subnet relationships.

Enable NSG Flow Logs per subnet NSG:

```
az network watcher flow-log configure \
  --resource-group NetworkRG \
  --nsg WebNSG \
```

```
--enabled true \
--storage-account mystorage \
--retention 30 \
--workspace
/subscriptions/.../resourceGroups/MonitoringRG/providers/Microsoft.O
perationalInsights/workspaces/loganalytics
```

These tools help ensure that your subnet design performs as intended and meets security standards.

Subnetting Best Practices

1. **Avoid subnet IP exhaustion**: Always plan for >20% unused IPs.

2. **Use naming conventions**: e.g., `subnet-prod-eastus-db`.

3. **Apply NSGs at the subnet level**: Enforce least privilege.

4. **Document subnet purposes**: Use tags and wikis.

5. **Test connectivity post-deployment**: Use tools like `az network watcher`.

6. **Reserve subnets for future services**: Private Endpoints, gateways.

7. **Apply UDRs consistently**: Avoid routing loops or dropped packets.

8. **Use small subnets in dev environments**: Save on IP space and cost.

9. **Enable logging early**: Helps troubleshoot from day one.

10. **Avoid mixing workload types**: Keep user VMs, platform services, and management in separate subnets.

Summary

Subnetting is far more than just slicing up IP ranges—it's a strategic activity that influences security, scalability, and operational efficiency. Azure offers extensive flexibility in subnet design, enabling tiered, role-based, and environment-based segmentation. Combined with NSGs, UDRs, service endpoints, and private links, subnets become a powerful mechanism to enforce enterprise-grade controls.

As you design your network, adopt a subnetting strategy aligned with your organizational architecture, compliance needs, and growth trajectory. Properly structured subnets improve fault isolation, enable consistent policy application, and pave the way for resilient and secure Azure deployments.

IP Address Management in Azure

IP address management (IPAM) is a critical aspect of designing, deploying, and operating Azure networking solutions. As environments grow in complexity—spanning multiple VNets, regions, services, and hybrid integrations—manual IP address tracking becomes unsustainable. Azure provides tools and methodologies to manage private and public IP address spaces effectively, enforce consistency, avoid collisions, and enable dynamic scalability. In this section, we'll cover private and public IP address types, allocation methods, reservation strategies, and best practices for enterprise-scale IP address management.

IP Address Fundamentals in Azure

Azure supports two main types of IP addresses:

- **Private IP addresses**: Used for internal communication within VNets and between peered   VNets.

- **Public IP addresses**: Enable inbound or outbound communication with the internet or external   services.

Both types can be:

- **Static**:   Manually   assigned   and   persistent.

- **Dynamic**: Assigned from a pool and can change (only private IPs can truly be dynamic).

Azure follows the RFC 1918 standard for private IP address ranges:

- `10.0.0.0`   `—`   `10.255.255.255`   `(/8)`

- `172.16.0.0`   `—`   `172.31.255.255`   `(/12)`

- `192.168.0.0`   `—`   `192.168.255.255`   `(/16)`

When designing your VNet, selecting a suitable range from these blocks is crucial for avoiding IP conflicts, especially in hybrid or multi-cloud deployments.

Private IP Address Management

Allocation Methods

In Azure, private IP addresses are allocated from a subnet's defined address range. Allocation happens when:

- A VM's network interface (NIC) is deployed.

- A private endpoint is created.

- A load balancer or gateway uses a frontend IP configuration.

There are two allocation methods:

- **Dynamic**: Azure assigns an available IP from the subnet pool. The IP may change when the NIC is deleted and recreated.

- **Static**: You specify the IP, and Azure reserves it until the NIC is deleted.

Assigning a static IP:

```
az network nic ip-config update \
  --name ipconfig1 \
  --nic-name myNic \
  --resource-group myResourceGroup \
  --private-ip-address 10.0.1.5
```

Dynamic IPs are suitable for general-purpose workloads, while static IPs are recommended for critical systems like domain controllers, firewalls, or DNS servers.

IP Reservation and Capacity Planning

Each subnet must be sized appropriately to avoid exhaustion. Azure reserves 5 IP addresses per subnet:

- Network address (first IP)

- Reserved by Azure for gateway (second–fourth IP)

- Broadcast address (last IP)

If you plan to scale workloads, estimate usage carefully. For example, an AKS node pool with 10 nodes and 30 pods each can consume hundreds of IPs.

Use address planning tools or spreadsheets to map allocations:

Subnet	CIDR	Usable IPs	Usage
WebSubnet	10.0.1.0/24	251	5 VMs, 1 Load Balancer

AppSubnet   10.0.2.0/24   251   3 VMs, 1 Private Endpoint

DBSubnet   10.0.3.0/26   59   2 VMs, reserved for growth

Tag and document IP usage to reduce conflicts and simplify troubleshooting.

Public IP Address Management

Public IP Types

Azure offers several public IP options:

- **Basic**: No zone redundancy, assigned from region-specific pools.

- **Standard**: Zone redundant, secure by default (requires NSG), supports availability zones.

Public IPs can also be:

- **Static**: Assigned permanently until manually released.

- **Dynamic**: Assigned temporarily; can change upon deallocation.

Example: Creating a static public IP:

```
az network public-ip create \
  --resource-group myResourceGroup \
  --name myPublicIP \
  --sku Standard \
  --allocation-method Static
```

Use cases for public IPs include:

- Inbound access to load balancers or application gateways.

- Outbound traffic using NAT gateway or load balancer SNAT.

- Jump boxes and VPN gateways.

DNS Labeling and FQDNs

Public IPs can be assigned a DNS label, which resolves to a fully qualified domain name (FQDN). This provides a user-friendly way to access services without needing to memorize IPs.

```
az network public-ip update \
  --resource-group myResourceGroup \
  --name myPublicIP \
  --dns-name myapp-dev-eastus
```

This creates a DNS name like `myapp-dev-eastus.eastus.cloudapp.azure.com`.

In production, consider using Azure DNS Zones or third-party DNS with custom domains.

NAT Gateway for Outbound IP Control

If you have multiple VMs or services that require consistent outbound IPs, consider using a NAT Gateway. It provides:

- Scalable outbound connectivity.

- Centralized IP control.

- Avoids SNAT port exhaustion on Standard Load Balancers.

Example: Assigning a NAT Gateway to a subnet

```
az network nat gateway create \
  --resource-group myResourceGroup \
  --name myNatGateway \
  --public-ip-addresses myPublicIP \
  --idle-timeout 10

az network vnet subnet update \
  --vnet-name myVNet \
  --name mySubnet \
  --resource-group myResourceGroup \
  --nat-gateway myNatGateway
```

This ensures all VMs in mySubnet use the same outbound public IP.

IP Addressing for Hybrid Connectivity

When connecting Azure to on-premises environments via VPN or ExpressRoute, overlapping IP ranges can cause routing issues. Follow these guidelines:

- Use non-overlapping, reserved CIDR blocks.

- Document on-prem and Azure address spaces clearly.

- For multi-region or multi-cloud, adopt a segmented IP block allocation model.

Example model:

Region	VNet Name	CIDR Block
East US	vnet-eastus	10.10.0.0/16
West Europe	vnet-westeu	10.20.0.0/16
On-prem	corp-dc	10.0.0.0/16

Avoid assigning 10.0.0.0/16 in Azure if it's already used on-premises.

You can use **Azure Private DNS** to resolve names instead of relying on IPs, which increases abstraction and flexibility.

Tools for IP Management

Azure doesn't yet offer a full-featured native IPAM (IP Address Management) tool, but you can build effective tracking and automation using:

- **Tags**: Assign metadata to resources.

- **Azure Resource Graph**: Query IP usage across the subscription.

- **PowerShell/CLI scripts**: Export used and available IPs.

- **Log Analytics**: Track failed deployments due to IP conflicts.

Sample query to get all IPs used by NICs:

```
az network nic list --query
"[].{name:name,ip:ipConfigurations[0].privateIpAddress}" -o table
```

Or using PowerShell:

```
Get-AzNetworkInterface          |          Select-Object          Name,
@{Name="IP";Expression={$_.IpConfigurations[0].PrivateIpAddress}}
```

For enterprise environments, consider integrating Azure with third-party IPAM tools like Infoblox, BlueCat, or SolarWinds for enhanced lifecycle management.

Automation of IP Assignment

In automated deployments, IPs can be:

- Assigned dynamically via ARM/Bicep

- Defined statically in IaC templates

Bicep example with static IP:

```
resource nic 'Microsoft.Network/networkInterfaces@2021-08-01' = {
  name: 'vmNic'
  location: location
  properties: {
    ipConfigurations: [
      {
        name: 'ipconfig1'
        properties: {
          privateIPAllocationMethod: 'Static'
          privateIPAddress: '10.1.1.5'
          subnet: {
            id: subnet.id
          }
        }
      }
    ]
  }
}
```

Use variables and parameter files to dynamically adjust IPs per environment.

Best Practices for IP Address Management

1. **Design address space hierarchically**: Region → VNet → Subnet → Host.

2. **Avoid small subnets**: Allow buffer space for growth and Azure reservations.

3. **Document everything**: Maintain an IP map or use Azure tagging standards.

4. **Use static IPs only when required**: Reduces overhead and conflicts.

5. **Integrate with IaC**: Ensure IP assignment is reproducible and version-controlled.

6. **Monitor usage**: Set alerts on IP exhaustion or failed deployments.

7. **Use NAT Gateway for predictable egress**: Avoid hidden SNAT behaviors.

8. **Plan for Private Link usage**: These consume IPs per service.

9. **Standardize DNS configuration**: Reduce IP dependencies in apps.

10. **Audit regularly**: Remove stale NICs or public IPs to reclaim space.

Summary

IP Address Management in Azure is a strategic discipline that directly impacts network performance, security, scalability, and operations. Whether you're working with private subnets, NAT gateways, hybrid scenarios, or Kubernetes clusters, understanding how IP addresses are allocated, reserved, and managed is crucial.

By combining careful planning with automation, tagging, and monitoring, you can avoid the most common pitfalls—such as subnet exhaustion, IP conflicts, and unexpected behavior during deployments. As your Azure footprint grows, solid IPAM practices will help ensure your network remains agile, secure, and future-ready.

Peering and VNet-to-VNet Connectivity

As Azure environments scale, there arises a need to connect multiple Virtual Networks (VNets) to share resources, enable service communication, support hybrid architectures, or enforce network segmentation. Azure VNet Peering and VNet-to-VNet connectivity options provide seamless and efficient mechanisms to establish these connections without complex routing or tunneling. This section covers in-depth how VNet Peering works, its design patterns, advanced configurations, and scenarios where peering is the ideal solution, along with alternatives like VPN-based connectivity.

Overview of VNet Peering

VNet Peering enables two virtual networks to communicate with each other using Azure's private backbone. Once peered, resources in each VNet can communicate as if they were on the same network.

Key characteristics:

- Low-latency, high-bandwidth connectivity.

- Uses Azure backbone (not public internet).

- Supports cross-region and same-region peering.

- Non-transitive by default (unless configured via hub-and-spoke).

- Can be configured across subscriptions and tenants.

Peering supports both intra-region (within the same Azure region) and global (cross-region) connectivity.

Use Cases for VNet Peering

- **Hub-and-spoke architectures**: Spokes peer to a shared hub for shared services like DNS, firewalls, or identity.

- **Environment separation**: Dev, test, and prod VNets that need controlled communication.

- **Business unit isolation**: Departments with separate VNets and subscriptions that still require interaction.

- **Cross-region redundancy**: Applications deployed in multiple regions for high availability.

VNet Peering is often preferred over site-to-site VPNs due to performance, simplicity, and cost (no VPN Gateway required).

Creating VNet Peering (Same Subscription, Same Region)

To peer two VNets within the same subscription:

1. Create two VNets (example: vnetA and vnetB).

2. Create peering from each VNet to the other.

```
az network vnet peering create \
  --name PeerToB \
  --resource-group RG1 \
  --vnet-name vnetA \
  --remote-vnet vnetB \
```

```
  --allow-vnet-access

az network vnet peering create \
  --name PeerToA \
  --resource-group RG1 \
  --vnet-name vnetB \
  --remote-vnet vnetA \
  --allow-vnet-access
```

For peering to work fully bidirectionally, both VNets must have peering defined pointing at each other.

Peering Across Subscriptions

If VNets reside in different subscriptions, you can still peer them—provided you have appropriate permissions.

Example:

```
az network vnet peering create \
  --name PeerToRemote \
  --resource-group RG1 \
  --vnet-name vnetA \
  --remote-vnet                          /subscriptions/xxxx-
xxxx/resourceGroups/RG2/providers/Microsoft.Network/virtualNetworks/
vnetB \
  --allow-vnet-access
```

You must have network contributor or owner permissions on both VNets to set up peering.

Global VNet Peering

Azure Global VNet Peering enables peering across regions. It is especially useful for:

- Multi-region   deployment   strategies.

- Connecting   regional   hubs.

- Distributing   users   or   services   across   geographies.

Example: Peering between East US and West Europe:

```
az network vnet peering create \
```

```
  --name EastToWest \
  --resource-group RG1 \
  --vnet-name vnet-eastus \
  --remote-vnet
/subscriptions/.../resourceGroups/RG2/providers/Microsoft.Network/vi
rtualNetworks/vnet-westeurope \
  --allow-vnet-access \
  --allow-forwarded-traffic \
  --allow-gateway-transit
```

Note that pricing for Global VNet Peering is higher than intra-region peering due to data transfer across regions.

Gateway Transit and Shared VPN Connectivity

In a hub-and-spoke model, the **hub VNet** often contains a VPN or ExpressRoute Gateway. **Gateway Transit** allows spoke VNets to use the hub's gateway for outbound or hybrid connectivity.

To enable gateway transit:

- The **hub VNet peering** must have `--allow-gateway-transit`.

- The **spoke VNet peering** must have `--use-remote-gateways`.

Hub side:

```
az network vnet peering update \
  --name Spoke1ToHub \
  --resource-group HubRG \
  --vnet-name hubVNet \
  --set allowGatewayTransit=true
```

Spoke side:

```
az network vnet peering update \
  --name HubToSpoke1 \
  --resource-group SpokeRG \
  --vnet-name spokeVNet \
  --set useRemoteGateways=true
```

Only one peering can use remote gateways per VNet. This is vital when centralizing connectivity.

Non-Transitive Nature of Peering

By default, peering is non-transitive:

- If VNet A is peered with B, and B is peered with C, A and C cannot communicate unless explicitly   peered.

- This design promotes intentionality and reduces risk of lateral movement.

To enable indirect communication, explicitly peer all involved VNets or use a transit VNet with a virtual appliance.

Routing and UDR Considerations

VNet Peering updates each VNet's route table with the remote VNet's address space, allowing seamless communication.

If you apply **User Defined Routes (UDRs)**, ensure they don't override the peering route unintentionally.

For example, if you force all 0.0.0.0/0 traffic to a firewall, ensure that peering subnets are excluded via more specific routes.

Network Security Group Implications

NSGs continue to apply as normal on peered traffic. Peering does **not** override or bypass NSG rules.

To allow traffic between peered VNets:

- Define   inbound   rules   on   target   resources'   NSGs.

- Ensure   source   IP   ranges   are   accounted   for.

For example, to allow AppSubnet in VNet B to access DBSubnet in VNet A:

```
az network nsg rule create \
  --resource-group RG1 \
  --nsg-name DBNSG \
  --name AllowAppToDB \
  --priority 100 \
  --direction Inbound \
  --access Allow \
```

```
--protocol Tcp \
--source-address-prefix 10.2.1.0/24 \
--destination-port-range 1433
```

This enforces traffic control even across peered VNets.

Monitoring Peering Connections

To monitor peered connections:

- Use **Network Watcher Topology** to visualize links.

- Review effective routes on NICs to confirm peering propagation.

- Enable **Activity Logs** to audit peering changes.

- Use **Azure Monitor Metrics** for bandwidth usage.

Example: View effective routes on a NIC:

```
az network nic show-effective-route-table \
  --name vmNic1 \
  --resource-group RG1
```

This helps verify that peering is injecting the correct routes.

Common Peering Architectures

Hub-and-Spoke Model

- Hub: Shared services (DNS, firewall, VPN)

- Spokes: App workloads, peered to hub

- Centralized inspection, logging, and management

Benefits:

- Policy enforcement

- Simplified connectivity

- Easier auditing and cost control

Mesh Peering

- Every VNet is peered with every other VNet.

- Suitable for small environments with full interconnectivity needs.

Drawbacks:

- Becomes unmanageable at scale.

- No transit routing unless explicitly configured.

Region Pairing

- Each application is deployed in two regions (for HA/DR).

- Peering is established across regional pairs.

This supports low-latency DR, replication, and failover.

Security Considerations

- Peering is internal to Azure but does not inherently encrypt traffic.

- Use **encryption at rest** and **TLS in transit** within applications.

- **NSGs and route tables** remain critical for enforcing controls.

- Enable **Azure Policy** to control peering permissions and enforce conventions.

- Tag peering resources to track purpose, environment, and owner.

Example policy: Deny peering unless it follows naming conventions:

```
{
  "if": {
    "allOf": [
      {
        "field": "type",
        "equals":
"Microsoft.Network/virtualNetworks/virtualNetworkPeerings"
      },
      {
        "not": {
```

```
        "field": "name",
        "like": "peer-*"
      }
    }
  ]
},
"then": {
  "effect": "deny"
}
}
```

Troubleshooting Peering Issues

- **Verify both peering directions exist**.

- **Check NSG rules**: Often the cause of blocked traffic.

- **Review route tables**: Ensure they don't override default routes.

- **Validate subnet IP ranges are non-overlapping**.

- **Check subscription permissions** if peering across boundaries.

- **Use Network Watcher Connection Monitor** for real-time testing.

Summary

VNet Peering is a cornerstone of modern Azure networking. It provides a scalable, high-performance, and secure way to interconnect virtual networks without requiring VPNs or internet traversal. Whether you're implementing a hub-and-spoke topology, enabling regional failover, or connecting workloads across environments, VNet Peering offers the simplicity and performance necessary for enterprise workloads.

By understanding its design principles, routing behavior, limitations, and integration points with gateways and NSGs, you can implement VNet-to-VNet connectivity that is robust, secure, and future-ready. As your environment evolves, VNet Peering becomes a powerful enabler of modular, service-oriented architecture in the cloud.

Chapter 3: Securing Azure Networks

Network Security Groups (NSGs) and Application Security Groups (ASGs)

Effective network security in Azure begins with the ability to control traffic flow to and from resources in a granular and scalable manner. Azure provides two powerful mechanisms for network-level access control: **Network Security Groups (NSGs)** and **Application Security Groups (ASGs)**. These constructs enable you to define, enforce, and manage inbound and outbound traffic rules across subnets and individual virtual machine interfaces (NICs), forming the backbone of network segmentation, micro-perimeter defenses, and Zero Trust networking strategies.

This section explores NSG and ASG architecture, configuration, best practices, integration patterns, and real-world scenarios to help you secure Azure networks from day one.

What Are Network Security Groups?

A **Network Security Group** is a layer-3 and layer-4 packet filtering firewall that allows or denies traffic based on:

- Source   and   destination   IP   addresses

- Source   and   destination   ports

- Protocol   (TCP,   UDP,   or   *   for   all)

- Direction   (inbound   or   outbound)

- Priority   (rule   evaluation   order)

NSGs are **stateful**, meaning that if an inbound rule allows traffic into a VM, the response is automatically allowed outbound, and vice versa.

NSGs can be associated with:

- **Subnets**:   All   NICs   in   the   subnet   inherit   the   rules.

- **Network   interfaces   (NICs)**:   Allows   per-resource   granularity.

Azure evaluates **NSG rules** in priority order (100–4096), with the lowest number taking precedence. Rules are additive but can be overridden by more specific matches.

NSG Default Rules

When you create an NSG, Azure includes three **default rules**:

Priority	Name	Direction	Action	Description
65000	AllowVnetInBound	Inbound	Allow	Traffic from same VNet
65001	AllowAzureLoadBalancerInBound	Inbound	Allow	From Azure load balancer
65500	DenyAllInbound	Inbound	Deny	All other inbound
65000	AllowVnetOutBound	Outbound	Allow	To same VNet
65001	AllowInternetOutBound	Outbound	Allow	To internet
65500	DenyAllOutbound	Outbound	Deny	All other outbound

These rules cannot be removed but are overridden by user-defined rules with higher precedence (lower numbers).

Creating and Managing NSGs

You can manage NSGs via Azure Portal, CLI, PowerShell, or Bicep. To create an NSG using the CLI:

```
az network nsg create \
  --resource-group SecureRG \
  --name WebNSG \
  --location eastus
```

To create an inbound rule allowing HTTP traffic from the internet:

```
az network nsg rule create \
  --resource-group SecureRG \
  --nsg-name WebNSG \
  --name AllowHTTP \
  --priority 100 \
  --direction Inbound \
  --access Allow \
  --protocol Tcp \
  --source-address-prefix Internet \
```

```
--destination-port-range 80
```

Associate the NSG with a subnet:

```
az network vnet subnet update \
  --vnet-name CorpVNet \
  --name WebSubnet \
  --resource-group SecureRG \
  --network-security-group WebNSG
```

Or with a specific NIC:

```
az network nic update \
  --name WebVMNic \
  --resource-group SecureRG \
  --network-security-group WebNSG
```

Inbound vs. Outbound Rules

Inbound Rules control traffic entering a resource from the network. Common scenarios:

- Allow HTTP/HTTPS to web servers
- Permit SQL traffic from application tier
- Enable RDP/SSH from jumpbox or admin IPs

Outbound Rules manage traffic leaving a resource. Example use cases:

- Restrict internet access
- Force outbound traffic through a firewall
- Allow DNS or update server access only

Outbound controls are often neglected but are critical in preventing data exfiltration or command-and-control traffic in compromised systems.

What Are Application Security Groups?

Application Security Groups (ASGs) provide **logical grouping** of VMs and NICs, simplifying NSG rule management in dynamic environments.

Instead of defining NSG rules with static IPs, you can target an ASG:

- Group NICs into **WebASG**, **AppASG**, **DBASG**, etc.

- Write NSG rules to allow traffic **from ASG to ASG**.

Benefits:

- Abstracts rule definitions from IP addresses.

- Auto-updates with resource membership changes.

- Reduces human error in large-scale environments.

To create an ASG:

```
az network asg create \
  --resource-group SecureRG \
  --name WebASG \
  --location eastus
```

Associate a VM NIC with the ASG:

```
az network nic update \
  --resource-group SecureRG \
  --name WebVMNic \
  --application-security-groups WebASG
```

Now define an NSG rule targeting the ASG:

```
az network nsg rule create \
  --resource-group SecureRG \
  --nsg-name AppNSG \
  --name AllowWebToApp \
  --priority 200 \
  --direction Inbound \
  --access Allow \
  --protocol Tcp \
  --source-asgs WebASG \
  --destination-asgs AppASG \
  --destination-port-range 443
```

This rule allows all NICs in `WebASG` to access those in `AppASG` on port 443.

NSG and ASG Integration Patterns

Microsegmentation

Divide your VNet into smaller zones using subnets and ASGs. Apply NSGs to enforce traffic rules:

- Subnet-based segmentation for environments (dev, test, prod).

- ASG-based segmentation for application tiers.

Hub-and-Spoke

- Apply NSGs on spoke subnets.

- Group spokes by purpose using ASGs (e.g., all VMs using shared services).

- Allow only required traffic from spoke ASGs to hub ASGs.

Jumpbox-Only Access

Create an `AdminASG` for NICs attached to jumpboxes. Use NSGs to allow RDP/SSH traffic **only** from AdminASG:

```
az network nsg rule create \
  --resource-group SecureRG \
  --nsg-name TargetNSG \
  --name AllowJumpbox \
  --priority 120 \
  --direction Inbound \
  --access Allow \
  --protocol Tcp \
  --source-asgs AdminASG \
  --destination-port-range 22
```

Logging and Monitoring NSG Activity

NSG Flow Logs are invaluable for visibility into allowed and denied traffic. Enable flow logs using Network Watcher:

```
az network watcher flow-log configure \
  --resource-group SecureRG \
```

```
    --nsg-name WebNSG \
    --enabled true \
    --storage-account mystorage \
    --traffic-analytics true \
    --workspace
/subscriptions/.../resourceGroups/.../providers/Microsoft.Operationa
lInsights/workspaces/myLogAnalytics
```

You can analyze traffic patterns, detect misconfigurations, or identify potential breaches.

Use **Azure Monitor Alerts** to be notified when rules change or unexpected traffic flows occur.

NSG and ASG Best Practices

1. **Use ASGs for flexibility**: Reduce static rule maintenance.

2. **Apply NSGs at subnet level for uniform policies**; at NIC level for overrides.

3. **Avoid open 0.0.0.0/0 unless necessary**: Use specific ranges or ASGs.

4. **Separate NSGs by tier or function**: Avoid monolithic rule sets.

5. **Review default NSG rules regularly**: Custom rules may override them.

6. **Document NSG rules and ASG usage**: For audit and compliance.

7. **Name NSGs/ASGs clearly**: E.g., `nsg-web-prod-eastus`, `asg-backend-apps`.

8. **Tag and track**: Use tags like `Environment=Prod`, `Tier=Web` for visibility.

9. **Use lower priorities for critical rules**: High-priority rules override others.

10. **Regularly audit flow logs**: Adjust NSGs based on actual traffic patterns.

Advanced Scenarios

Integration with Azure Firewall

NSGs and ASGs can work in tandem with **Azure Firewall**. For example:

- NSGs allow traffic from trusted sources.
- UDRs route traffic to Azure Firewall.

- Azure Firewall applies L7 inspection and threat intelligence.

This layered defense enhances both perimeter and host-level security.

Controlling Intra-Subnet Traffic

By default, VMs in the same subnet can communicate. To restrict this:

- Apply NSG to deny traffic from **virtualNetwork** to **virtualNetwork**.

- Use ASGs to allow selective intra-subnet communication.

Example rule to deny all intra-subnet traffic except WebASG to AppASG:

```
# Deny intra-subnet
az network nsg rule create \
  --resource-group SecureRG \
  --nsg-name WebNSG \
  --name DenyIntraSubnet \
  --priority 300 \
  --direction Inbound \
  --access Deny \
  --protocol '*' \
  --source-address-prefix VirtualNetwork \
  --destination-address-prefix VirtualNetwork

# Allow Web to App
az network nsg rule create \
  --resource-group SecureRG \
  --nsg-name WebNSG \
  --name AllowWebToApp \
  --priority 200 \
  --direction Inbound \
  --access Allow \
  --protocol Tcp \
  --source-asgs WebASG \
  --destination-asgs AppASG \
  --destination-port-range 443
```

Summary

Network Security Groups and Application Security Groups are the bedrock of access control in Azure virtual networks. NSGs provide stateful, packet-level filtering to subnets and NICs, while ASGs abstract the complexity of IP-based targeting and bring agility to dynamic environments.

By combining NSGs with ASGs, organizations can implement granular, scalable, and auditable network policies that align with Zero Trust, compliance, and segmentation goals. Whether you're securing a single workload or architecting a multi-tenant, hybrid cloud platform, mastering NSGs and ASGs is essential to protecting your Azure network from evolving threats and unauthorized access.

Implementing Azure Firewall

Azure Firewall is a cloud-native, intelligent, and scalable network security service that provides stateful traffic inspection, high availability, and threat intelligence for your Azure environments. Unlike Network Security Groups (NSGs) which operate at the network interface and subnet levels, Azure Firewall is deployed centrally and inspects both inbound and outbound traffic at the perimeter. It is ideal for implementing a centralized security model in hub-and-spoke or hybrid cloud architectures.

This section will guide you through Azure Firewall's features, configuration, deployment models, integration strategies, and advanced use cases. It is intended to provide the depth necessary to understand how Azure Firewall fits into enterprise-grade cloud security architectures.

Azure Firewall Overview

Azure Firewall is a fully managed service that operates at Layer 3–7 of the OSI model. It provides:

- **Stateful packet inspection**: Remembers session state across connections.

- **Application rule filtering**: FQDN-based filtering for HTTP/S traffic.

- **Network rule filtering**: Protocol, IP, and port-based filtering.

- **Threat intelligence**: Blocks traffic to/from known malicious IPs and domains.

- **Logging and analytics**: Deep integration with Azure Monitor and Log Analytics.

- **High availability and scalability**: Built-in redundancy and support for scaling throughput with Azure Firewall Premium.

Azure Firewall is often deployed in the **hub** of a hub-and-spoke topology, where all traffic from spoke VNets and on-premises networks is routed for inspection.

SKU Comparison: Standard vs. Premium

Azure Firewall is offered in two SKUs:

Feature	Standard	Premium
Stateful traffic inspection	✓	✓
Threat intelligence	✓	✓
TLS inspection	✗	✓
IDPS	✗	✓
URL filtering	✗	✓
Web categories	✗	✓

Use **Premium** for highly regulated environments, especially those requiring TLS decryption and intrusion prevention capabilities.

Deployment Architecture

The typical architecture includes:

- **Azure Firewall subnet** (`AzureFirewallSubnet`): Must exist in the hub VNet.

- **Public IP address**: Assigned to the firewall for internet-bound traffic.

- **Route tables (UDRs)**: Force traffic from other subnets/spokes through the firewall.

- **Optional DNAT rules**: For publishing services to the internet.

This setup creates a central choke point where traffic is logged, filtered, and inspected before reaching its destination.

Creating Azure Firewall (CLI)

```
# Create a public IP
az network public-ip create \
  --name fw-pip \
  --resource-group HubRG \
  --sku Standard \
  --allocation-method Static
```

```
# Create the AzureFirewallSubnet
az network vnet subnet create \
  --name AzureFirewallSubnet \
  --resource-group HubRG \
  --vnet-name HubVNet \
  --address-prefix 10.0.100.0/24

# Create the firewall
az network firewall create \
  --name MyFirewall \
  --resource-group HubRG \
  --location eastus \
  --sku Standard

# Associate the public IP
az network firewall ip-config create \
  --firewall-name MyFirewall \
  --resource-group HubRG \
  --name FWConfig \
  --public-ip-address fw-pip \
  --vnet-name HubVNet
```

Once deployed, Azure Firewall becomes a routable hop for all traffic directed through UDRs.

Creating Rules

Azure Firewall uses three types of rules:

1. **Network Rules** – Protocol/port-based control.

2. **Application Rules** – FQDN and web-based control.

3. **NAT Rules** – Translate inbound public IPs to private endpoints.

Network Rule Example

```
az network firewall network-rule create \
  --firewall-name MyFirewall \
  --resource-group HubRG \
  --collection-name NetRules \
  --name AllowDNS \
  --rule-type NetworkRule \
```

```
  --action Allow \
  --priority 100 \
  --rule-name AllowDNS \
  --protocols UDP \
  --source-addresses 10.1.0.0/16 \
  --destination-addresses 168.63.129.16 \
  --destination-ports 53
```

Application Rule Example

```
az network firewall application-rule create \
  --firewall-name MyFirewall \
  --resource-group HubRG \
  --collection-name AppRules \
  --name AllowMicrosoft \
  --rule-type ApplicationRule \
  --action Allow \
  --priority 100 \
  --source-addresses 10.1.0.0/16 \
  --protocols Http=80 Https=443 \
  --target-fqdns '*.microsoft.com'
```

NAT Rule Example

```
az network firewall nat-rule create \
  --firewall-name MyFirewall \
  --resource-group HubRG \
  --collection-name DNATRules \
  --name WebInbound \
  --rule-type NatRule \
  --action Dnat \
  --priority 100 \
  --translated-address 10.1.1.4 \
  --translated-port 80 \
  --protocols TCP \
  --source-addresses '*' \
  --destination-addresses <FirewallPublicIP> \
  --destination-ports 80
```

These rules collectively control which traffic enters, leaves, or transits through your environment.

Route Tables and Traffic Redirection

To ensure traffic flows through Azure Firewall, create UDRs and associate them with subnets or VNet peering routes.

Example UDR to redirect internet-bound traffic:

```
az network route-table create \
  --name WebRouteTable \
  --resource-group AppRG

az network route-table route create \
  --name DefaultToFirewall \
  --resource-group AppRG \
  --route-table-name WebRouteTable \
  --address-prefix 0.0.0.0/0 \
  --next-hop-type VirtualAppliance \
  --next-hop-ip-address 10.0.100.4

az network vnet subnet update \
  --vnet-name AppVNet \
  --name WebSubnet \
  --resource-group AppRG \
  --route-table WebRouteTable
```

This ensures all outbound traffic from the subnet flows through the firewall.

Logging and Monitoring

Azure Firewall logs all allowed and denied traffic through **Azure Monitor** and **Log Analytics**.

Enable diagnostics:

```
az monitor diagnostic-settings create \
  --name FWLogs \
  --resource-id $(az network firewall show --name MyFirewall --resource-group HubRG --query id -o tsv) \
  --workspace <log-analytics-id> \
  --logs '[{"category": "AzureFirewallNetworkRule", "enabled": true}, {"category": "AzureFirewallApplicationRule", "enabled": true}]'
```

Use **Kusto queries** in Log Analytics to analyze traffic, identify anomalies, and create alerts.

Example query to find blocked traffic:

```
AzureDiagnostics
| where Category == "AzureFirewallNetworkRule"
| where action_s == "Deny"
| project TimeGenerated, src_ip_s, dst_ip_s, protocol_s, rule_name_s
```

Advanced Scenarios

TLS Inspection

In **Premium SKU**, Azure Firewall can decrypt and inspect TLS traffic, offering visibility into encrypted sessions.

- Requires uploading a trusted root CA certificate.

- Can define rules based on SNI and URL categories.

- Enables detection of malicious or non-compliant HTTPS traffic.

Intrusion Detection and Prevention (IDPS)

Also exclusive to Premium SKU, IDPS:

- Detects threats like port scans, SQL injections, and exploits.

- Provides detection mode or prevention mode.

- Integrates with alerts and Defender for Cloud.

Web Category Filtering

Allows rule definitions based on predefined categories like:

- Social media

- Gambling

- Malware

- High bandwidth

Example application rule:

```
az network firewall application-rule create \
```

```
--firewall-name MyFirewall \
--resource-group HubRG \
--collection-name WebBlockRules \
--name BlockGambling \
--rule-type ApplicationRule \
--action Deny \
--priority 200 \
--source-addresses 10.1.0.0/16 \
--protocols Https=443 \
--web-categories "Gambling"
```

This is especially valuable in compliance-focused environments like finance or government.

Integration with Hub-and-Spoke and Hybrid Models

Azure Firewall is ideal for **centralizing security** in a **hub-and-spoke topology**:

- Hub contains the firewall and shared services.

- Spokes connect via peering with **Use Remote Gateways** set.

- UDRs route all egress through the hub's firewall.

In hybrid scenarios, traffic from on-premises networks via **VPN Gateway** or **ExpressRoute** can be routed through Azure Firewall for inspection before reaching Azure workloads.

This approach enables:

- Centralized logging and alerting.

- Uniform threat intelligence enforcement.

- Simplified management.

Best Practices

1. **Deploy in a dedicated subnet** named `AzureFirewallSubnet`.

2. **Use Premium SKU** for regulated workloads requiring deep inspection.

3. **Define clear rule collections** (App, Net, NAT) and document them.

4. **Enable diagnostics** from day one to ensure visibility.

5. **Tag firewall resources** for identification and cost tracking.

6. **Test rules before deploying to production** using NSG Flow Logs and diagnostics.

7. **Use policy-based routing** for granular traffic control.

8. **Combine with Defender for Cloud** for enhanced security posture.

9. **Back up configuration regularly** using templates or automation.

10. **Monitor metrics** like SNAT port exhaustion or high latency.

Summary

Azure Firewall provides a robust, cloud-native, and centralized approach to securing Azure network traffic. It complements NSGs and ASGs by acting as a perimeter security device capable of deep inspection, application awareness, and comprehensive logging. Whether you're building a secure enterprise network, enforcing compliance policies, or consolidating security management, Azure Firewall delivers the scalability, intelligence, and simplicity required in modern cloud deployments.

By understanding its deployment models, rule architecture, advanced capabilities, and best practices, you can implement a firewall strategy that protects your infrastructure today and scales with your needs tomorrow.

Distributed Denial-of-Service (DDoS) Protection

Distributed Denial-of-Service (DDoS) attacks are among the most disruptive and pervasive threats in today's digital landscape. These attacks aim to overwhelm services with a flood of illegitimate traffic, causing resource exhaustion, downtime, degraded performance, or even complete service disruption. As enterprises migrate critical infrastructure to the cloud, including customer-facing applications and internal services, protecting against DDoS attacks becomes essential for availability, resilience, and brand reputation.

Microsoft Azure offers **built-in DDoS protection** for all customers and an enhanced service tier, **Azure DDoS Protection Standard**, designed to deliver enterprise-grade defense against volumetric, protocol, and resource-layer attacks. This section explores DDoS concepts, Azure's DDoS protection services, configuration procedures, detection and mitigation mechanisms, integration with monitoring tools, and best practices for maintaining strong DDoS defenses.

What Is a DDoS Attack?

A Distributed Denial-of-Service (DDoS) attack uses multiple sources, often a botnet, to flood a target system or network with traffic or requests, making it unavailable to legitimate users. These attacks typically fall into three categories:

1. **Volumetric Attacks**: Attempt to consume bandwidth with a flood of packets or requests (e.g., UDP floods, ICMP floods).

2. **Protocol Attacks**: Exploit weaknesses in network layer protocols (e.g., SYN floods, fragmented packets).

3. **Application Layer Attacks**: Target web applications and services with malformed or excessive requests (e.g., HTTP floods).

DDoS attacks can affect:

- Virtual machines (VMs)
- Public IP addresses
- Load balancers
- Application gateways
- Public-facing APIs and endpoints

Azure's Approach to DDoS Protection

Azure provides two layers of DDoS protection:

1. Basic DDoS Protection (Included by Default)

- Automatically enabled for all Azure services.
- Protects against common network-level attacks.
- No user configuration required.
- Utilizes Azure's global network presence and mitigation pipeline.
- Shared across tenants in a multitenant defense.

This is sufficient for low-risk or internal-only environments but lacks alerting, reports, and configuration controls.

2. Azure DDoS Protection Standard (Paid SKU)

- Applies to **public IPs** attached to Azure resources.
- Offers **always-on traffic monitoring**.

- Automatically mitigates attacks based on adaptive tuning.
- Includes **DDoS Rapid Response (DRR)** support.
- Generates **detailed telemetry, logging, and alerts**.
- Offers **cost protection** for attack-related service overages.

DDoS Protection Standard is the recommended choice for production workloads, especially those that are publicly accessible or mission-critical.

Enabling Azure DDoS Protection Standard

DDoS Protection Standard is enabled at the **virtual network (VNet)** level. Once enabled, it automatically protects all public IPs associated with resources in that VNet.

Step 1: Create a DDoS Protection Plan

```
az network ddos-protection create \
  --resource-group SecureRG \
  --name DDoSPlan
```

Step 2: Associate the Plan with a VNet

```
az network vnet update \
  --name ProdVNet \
  --resource-group ProdRG \
  --ddos-protection-plan DDoSPlan \
  --enable-ddos-protection true
```

Once associated, Azure applies DDoS Protection to **all public IPs** in that VNet, such as those on VMs, load balancers, or application gateways.

Step 3: Verify the Association

```
az network vnet show \
  --name ProdVNet \
  --resource-group ProdRG \
  --query "ddosProtectionPlan"
```

How Azure DDoS Protection Works

Azure DDoS Protection monitors inbound traffic continuously using machine learning to identify normal baselines and detect anomalies. When an attack is detected:

- Traffic is redirected through the DDoS mitigation pipeline.

- Malicious traffic is dropped or throttled.

- Legitimate traffic continues to flow without interruption.

Mitigation happens automatically and does not require manual intervention.

The service protects against:

- SYN/ACK floods

- DNS reflection

- UDP amplification

- TCP connection exhaustion

- Application layer bursts

Integration with Monitoring and Alerts

DDoS Protection Standard integrates with **Azure Monitor**, **Log Analytics**, and **Microsoft Defender for Cloud** to provide visibility into attack activity and mitigations.

Enabling Diagnostics

```
az monitor diagnostic-settings create \
  --name DDoSLogs \
  --resource $(az network ddos-protection show --name DDoSPlan --
resource-group SecureRG --query id -o tsv) \
  --workspace
/subscriptions/.../resourceGroups/SecureRG/providers/Microsoft.Opera
tionalInsights/workspaces/MyLogAnalytics \
  --logs '[{"category": "DDoSMitigationFlowLogs","enabled": true}]'
```

Sample Kusto Query: View Recent Attacks

```
AzureDiagnostics
| where Category == "DDoSMitigationFlowLogs"
| summarize Count = count() by bin(TimeGenerated, 1h), attackVector_s,
mitigationReason_s
```

Configuring Alerts

Use Azure Monitor alert rules to get notified when:

- An attack is detected.

- A mitigation starts or ends.

- Specific IPs are targeted.

Alerts can be sent via email, SMS, webhook, or integrated into a SIEM like Sentinel.

DDoS Rapid Response (DRR)

For high-severity attacks, **Microsoft's DDoS Rapid Response team** can be engaged to assist in real-time attack analysis and custom mitigation.

DRR can help with:

- Attack diagnostics

- Traffic analysis

- Support escalation

- Post-incident review

DRR is available to all customers with DDoS Protection Standard.

Cost Protection Feature

Azure offers **cost protection** as part of DDoS Standard. This ensures that:

- Service overages (e.g., bandwidth, scale-up resources) directly resulting from a documented DDoS attack may be **credited**.

- Eligible customers must submit a support request with proof of attack via logs and mitigation reports.

This is an important benefit for organizations with strict budget governance or regulatory cost constraints.

Best Practices for DDoS Resilience

1. **Enable DDoS Standard for public-facing workloads**: Don't rely solely on Basic protection for critical services.

2. **Combine DDoS Protection with Azure Web Application Firewall (WAF)** for L7 filtering.

3. **Deploy behind Load Balancers or Application Gateways**: These help distribute load and absorb bursts.

4. **Use Rate Limiting and Throttling**: Apply at app/API layer to protect from HTTP floods.

5. **Geo-block unnecessary regions**: Reduce attack surface using NSGs or WAF rules.

6. **Monitor and baseline normal traffic**: Use Azure Monitor and Flow Logs.

7. **Plan for scale-out under attack**: Ensure auto-scaling policies are conservative and cost-aware.

8. **Run DDoS simulation tests** (via third-party services) in non-production environments to validate architecture.

9. **Harden public APIs** with authentication, CAPTCHA, and input validation.

10. **Keep contact and escalation info ready** for DRR engagement in critical situations.

Advanced Scenarios

Multi-Region Applications

If your application spans regions, enable DDoS Protection in each region's VNet containing public IPs.

- Protects regional failover paths.

- Enables parallel mitigation across availability zones.

Hybrid Connectivity

While DDoS Standard protects Azure public IPs, it does not extend to on-prem IPs. However, Azure-native services connected over VPN or ExpressRoute can still benefit from DDoS defense at the Azure ingress.

For shared services or centralized routing models, protect the **hub VNet** to cover all spokes routing internet-bound traffic through the hub.

Paired with Azure Firewall

Using Azure Firewall with DDoS Protection Standard creates a layered defense:

- **DDoS** handles volumetric and protocol-layer attacks.

- **Azure Firewall** inspects packet payloads, enforces allow/deny rules, and logs detailed analytics.

This combination is ideal for enterprises subject to compliance or regulatory mandates (e.g., PCI-DSS, ISO 27001).

Summary

Distributed Denial-of-Service attacks pose a persistent threat to application availability and customer trust. With Azure DDoS Protection—particularly the Standard SKU—organizations gain access to intelligent, adaptive, and automated defense mechanisms that scale with the complexity and traffic volume of modern cloud applications.

By enabling DDoS Protection Standard, associating it with public-facing VNets, and integrating its telemetry with monitoring and incident response workflows, you can substantially reduce your exposure to downtime and data loss. When combined with other security tools like Azure Firewall and Web Application Firewall, Azure DDoS Protection forms a critical layer of defense in a comprehensive cloud security strategy.

Best Practices for Access Control and Segmentation

Access control and network segmentation are fundamental components of any secure cloud architecture. In Microsoft Azure, they enable you to limit traffic flows, reduce the blast radius of a potential breach, enforce regulatory compliance, and maintain tenant or workload isolation. Effective implementation of these strategies prevents lateral movement within a compromised network, enables fine-grained permission management, and ensures that only necessary communications are permitted between resources, applications, and services.

This section provides a comprehensive guide to designing and enforcing access control and segmentation in Azure using a combination of platform-native tools including Network Security Groups (NSGs), Application Security Groups (ASGs), Route Tables (UDRs), firewalls, and Azure policies. It also explores practical patterns for microsegmentation, service exposure minimization, and Zero Trust networking.

Principles of Access Control in Azure

Access control in Azure operates on two primary axes:

1. **Network Access Control** – Governs data-plane traffic between resources using mechanisms such as NSGs, ASGs, Azure Firewall, UDRs, and VNet Peering.

2. **Identity-based Access Control** – Governs control-plane access (who can manage what) using Azure Active Directory (AAD) and Role-Based Access Control (RBAC).

This section focuses primarily on network access control—i.e., **what network traffic is allowed or denied**, where it originates, and where it's going.

Key principles:

- **Least Privilege**: Grant only the minimum access required.

- **Explicit Deny**: Block by default; allow only specific, necessary traffic.

- **Microsegmentation**: Segment workloads and networks at a granular level.

- **East-West Isolation**: Prevent lateral movement between VMs/services in the same region or environment.

- **Environment Separation**: Isolate dev, test, and production workloads.

Network Segmentation Models

Azure enables multiple segmentation strategies:

1. Subnet-based Segmentation

Each subnet is a broadcast domain and can have its own NSG, route table, and access policies.

Example layout:

- `10.0.1.0/24`   —   Web   Tier

- `10.0.2.0/24`   —   Application   Tier

- `10.0.3.0/24`   —   Database   Tier

Apply NSGs to each subnet to enforce which subnets may communicate with each other.

```
az network nsg rule create \
  --resource-group SecureRG \
  --nsg-name AppNSG \
  --name AllowWebToApp \
  --priority 100 \
  --direction Inbound \
  --access Allow \
  --protocol Tcp \
  --source-address-prefix 10.0.1.0/24 \
  --destination-port-range 443
```

All other traffic is implicitly denied unless allowed.

2. ASG-based Logical Segmentation

Application Security Groups (ASGs) abstract the segmentation model by allowing you to group resources logically (e.g., by function or role).

Example:

- `asg-web` — All web servers

- `asg-app` — Application servers

- `asg-db` — Databases

NSG rules can target ASGs instead of IP ranges:

```
az network nsg rule create \
  --resource-group SecureRG \
  --nsg-name DBNSG \
  --name AllowAppToDB \
  --priority 110 \
  --direction Inbound \
  --access Allow \
  --protocol Tcp \
  --source-asgs asg-app \
  --destination-asgs asg-db \
  --destination-port-range 1433
```

This enables dynamic updates as servers are added or removed from the group.

3. Hub-and-Spoke Segmentation

A centralized **hub VNet** hosts shared services (e.g., DNS, firewalls, VPNs), while **spoke VNets** host applications or workloads. Traffic is routed through the hub using VNet peering and UDRs.

Benefits:

- Centralized inspection/logging.

- Simplified routing control.

- Reduced surface area.

Each spoke can have its own NSGs and ASGs, and the hub may contain Azure Firewall for advanced control.

Zero Trust Network Access (ZTNA)

Zero Trust assumes that no network, internal or external, is inherently trusted. Every request must be verified explicitly.

Key strategies:

- **Deny by default at all layers.**
- **Strong identity validation (AAD, managed identities).**
- **Multi-factor authentication (MFA).**
- **Policy-based conditional access.**
- **Encryption in transit and at rest.**
- **Continuous monitoring and audit logging.**

ZTNA in Azure is implemented through:

- **NSGs and ASGs for microsegmentation.**
- **Private Link to eliminate public exposure.**
- **Just-in-Time (JIT) VM Access.**
- **Conditional Access and RBAC.**
- **Azure Firewall with TLS inspection.**

Access Control with NSGs and ASGs

Subnet-Level Isolation

Deploy NSGs at the subnet level to enforce environment boundaries. For example:

- Deny all internet access on backend subnets.
- Allow only specific ports from defined source subnets.

```
az network nsg rule create \
  --resource-group SecureRG \
  --nsg-name BackendNSG \
  --name DenyInternet \
  --priority 100 \
  --direction Outbound \
  --access Deny \
  --protocol "*" \
  --destination-address-prefix Internet \
  --destination-port-range "*"
```

Host-Level Overrides

NSGs can also be applied directly to NICs, overriding subnet rules. This is useful for jumpboxes or exceptions.

Using ASGs to Replace IP-Based Rules

Replace brittle IP-based rules with logical groups:

- Easier   maintenance.

- No   IP   tracking   required.

- Scales   with   dynamic   infrastructure   (VMSS,   AKS).

```
az network nic update \
  --resource-group SecureRG \
  --name WebVMNic01 \
  --application-security-groups asg-web
```

User Defined Routes (UDRs) for Traffic Flow Control

Use UDRs to:

- Force   traffic   through   Azure   Firewall   or   NVA.

- Segment   routing   paths   per   workload   or   subnet.

- Deny   or   isolate   certain   communication   paths.

Example: Force all outbound traffic through a firewall:

```
az network route-table route create \
  --name DefaultRoute \
  --resource-group SecureRG \
  --route-table-name SpokeRouteTable \
  --address-prefix 0.0.0.0/0 \
  --next-hop-type VirtualAppliance \
  --next-hop-ip-address 10.0.0.4
```

Apply the route table to the subnet:

```
az network vnet subnet update \
  --vnet-name SpokeVNet \
  --name WebSubnet \
  --resource-group SecureRG \
  --route-table SpokeRouteTable
```

Combine UDRs with NSGs to build robust traffic control planes.

Private Link for Minimizing Exposure

Azure Private Link allows private access to PaaS services from within your VNet using private IPs. This eliminates public endpoint exposure.

- Use for Storage, SQL, Key Vault, Cosmos DB, and more.

- Combine with NSG/ASG to limit access to only specific hosts or tiers.

Private Link Subnets should be isolated with NSGs that **deny all inbound** traffic except known source ASGs.

```
az network private-endpoint create \
  --name kv-pe \
  --resource-group SecureRG \
  --vnet-name HubVNet \
  --subnet PrivateEndpointSubnet \
  --private-connection-resource-id /subscriptions/.../vaults/mykv \
  --group-ids vault
```

Identity-Based Controls

While this section focuses on network access, it's critical to pair it with identity controls:

- **Azure AD Conditional Access**: Enforce access based on user/device/location.

- **RBAC**: Ensure only authorized admins can change NSG rules or route tables.

- **Privileged Identity Management (PIM)**: Grant time-bound access to sensitive resources.

Example: Assign read-only access to a network admin:

```
az role assignment create \
  --assignee admin@company.com \
  --role Reader \
  --scope /subscriptions/xxxx-xxxx/resourceGroups/SecureRG
```

Monitoring and Auditing Access Controls

Use the following tools for visibility:

- **NSG Flow Logs**: View real-time traffic flows.

- **Azure Monitor Logs**: Query and alert on rule hits or denials.

- **Change History**: Detect rule or route table changes via Activity Logs.

- **Microsoft Defender for Cloud**: Audit compliance and recommend hardening.

Sample Kusto query to detect denied traffic:

```
AzureDiagnostics
| where Category == "NetworkSecurityGroupFlowEvent"
| where action_s == "D"
| summarize count() by src_ip_s, dest_ip_s, dest_port_s, rule_s
```

Set alerts on unauthorized changes to NSGs:

```
az monitor activity-log alert create \
  --name NSGChangeAlert \
  --resource-group SecureRG \
  --condition "category=Administrative and
operationName=Microsoft.Network/networkSecurityGroups/write" \
  --action-group MyAlertGroup
```

Best Practices for Access Control and Segmentation

1. **Start with deny-by-default**: Only allow what's explicitly needed.

2. **Segment by function and environment**: Web, app, and data tiers should be separated.

3. **Use ASGs instead of static IPs**: Improves agility and reduces maintenance.

4. **Apply NSGs at the subnet level**: Enforces uniform policy across deployments.

5. **Inspect and log traffic**: Use Azure Firewall, NSG Flow Logs, and Log Analytics.

6. **Minimize public exposure**: Prefer Private Link and service endpoints.

7. **Restrict east-west traffic**: Deny intra-subnet communication unless required.

8. **Use UDRs to direct traffic**: Centralize inspection through firewalls.

9. **Combine network and identity controls**: Implement layered defense.

10. **Automate and audit continuously**: Use ARM, Bicep, or Terraform for IaC, and enable change monitoring.

Summary

Access control and segmentation are foundational to a secure Azure deployment. With NSGs, ASGs, UDRs, Private Link, and firewall integration, Azure offers a rich set of tools for building secure, segmented, and policy-compliant networks. By adopting Zero Trust principles, segmenting by environment or role, and enforcing fine-grained traffic rules, you reduce risk, ensure operational continuity, and meet organizational and regulatory security goals.

As environments scale and diversify, strong access control becomes not only a security necessity but an enabler of cloud agility and resilience.

Chapter 4: Hybrid Network Architectures

Connecting On-Premises to Azure: VPN and ExpressRoute

In many real-world scenarios, organizations cannot immediately move all their workloads to the cloud. A hybrid networking architecture allows businesses to extend their on-premises data centers into the Azure cloud while maintaining a consistent and secure networking experience. Azure provides two primary connectivity options for this: **Site-to-Site VPN** and **ExpressRoute**. This section explores both options in depth, outlines use cases, and provides guidance on choosing between them.

Understanding Hybrid Networking in Azure

Hybrid networks bridge the gap between on-premises infrastructure and cloud services. These architectures are vital in scenarios such as:

- Gradual migration of workloads to Azure

- Disaster recovery and business continuity planning

- Compliance with regulations that require data locality

- Leveraging Azure for development and testing while production remains on-premises

Azure enables hybrid connectivity using either the public internet (via VPN) or dedicated connections (via ExpressRoute), both of which support secure communication with encryption and authentication mechanisms.

Site-to-Site VPN: Overview and Configuration

A **Site-to-Site (S2S) VPN** provides an IPsec/IKE (IKEv1 or IKEv2) tunnel between the on-premises VPN device and Azure. This solution is relatively easy to set up, cost-effective, and ideal for smaller or temporary workloads.

Key Components:

- **Virtual Network Gateway**: A gateway type VPN, configured in a specific subnet called the GatewaySubnet.

- **On-premises VPN device**: A physical or software device that supports IPsec/IKE.

- **Local Network Gateway**: Defines your on-premises network address space and public   IP.

Step-by-Step: Configuring Site-to-Site VPN

1. Create a Virtual Network and GatewaySubnet

```
az network vnet create \
  --name MyVNet \
  --resource-group MyResourceGroup \
  --location eastus \
  --address-prefix 10.1.0.0/16 \
  --subnet-name GatewaySubnet \
  --subnet-prefix 10.1.255.0/27
```

2. Create a Public IP for the Gateway

```
az network public-ip create \
  --resource-group MyResourceGroup \
  --name VNetGatewayIP \
  --allocation-method Dynamic
```

3. Create the Virtual Network Gateway

```
az network vnet-gateway create \
  --name MyVNetGateway \
  --resource-group MyResourceGroup \
  --vnet MyVNet \
  --public-ip-address VNetGatewayIP \
  --gateway-type Vpn \
  --vpn-type RouteBased \
  --sku VpnGw1 \
  --no-wait
```

4. Define the Local Network Gateway

```
az network local-gateway create \
  --name MyLocalNetworkGateway \
  --resource-group MyResourceGroup \
  --gateway-ip-address <ON_PREMISES_PUBLIC_IP> \
```

```
--local-address-prefixes <ON_PREMISES_ADDRESS_SPACE>
```

5. Create the VPN Connection

```
az network vpn-connection create \
  --name MyConnection \
  --resource-group MyResourceGroup \
  --vnet-gateway1 MyVNetGateway \
  --local-gateway2 MyLocalNetworkGateway \
  --shared-key 'MySecretKey123!'
```

Pros and Use Cases:

- Quick to implement

- Suitable for remote offices or small branches

- Great for DR and backup scenarios

Limitations:

- Performance depends on internet connection

- Not suitable for low-latency or high-throughput workloads

ExpressRoute: Private and High-Performance Connectivity

Azure ExpressRoute provides a private connection between your on-premises network and Microsoft Azure data centers. This is not done over the public internet, resulting in more reliability, faster speeds, and consistent latencies.

Key Features:

- Layer 3 connectivity through Ethernet exchange providers or point-to-point Ethernet connections

- Supports bandwidths up to 100 Gbps

- Option to connect to Microsoft 365 services

- Integration with Azure Private Peering and Microsoft Peering

ExpressRoute Circuit Configuration

Unlike VPNs, ExpressRoute circuits are set up with the help of a connectivity provider. Here's how to configure the Azure part of an ExpressRoute circuit:

1. Create an ExpressRoute Circuit

```
az network express-route create \
  --name MyERCircuit \
  --resource-group MyResourceGroup \
  --bandwidth 200 \
  --provider "Equinix" \
  --peering-location "Silicon Valley" \
  --sku-tier Standard \
  --sku-family MeteredData
```

2. View Service Key and Share with Provider

```
az network express-route show \
  --name MyERCircuit \
  --resource-group MyResourceGroup \
  --query serviceKey
```

This service key is shared with the connectivity provider to complete the provisioning on their end.

3. Configure Peering (Private Peering example)

```
az network express-route peering create \
  --circuit-name MyERCircuit \
  --resource-group MyResourceGroup \
  --peering-type AzurePrivatePeering \
  --peer-asn 65010 \
  --primary-peer-subnet 192.168.1.0/30 \
  --secondary-peer-subnet 192.168.2.0/30 \
  --vlan-id 200
```

Pros and Use Cases:

- Highly secure, as traffic does not traverse the public internet

- Predictable   performance

- Meets compliance for many regulatory frameworks

- Ideal for large enterprises, financial institutions, and government bodies

Limitations:

- Higher cost compared to VPN

- Requires working with a network provider

- More complex to implement and manage

Choosing Between VPN and ExpressRoute

Criteria	Site-to-Site VPN	ExpressRoute
Cost	Low	High
Performance	Moderate (depends on ISP)	High (dedicated bandwidth)
Security	Encrypted over internet	Private, secure connection
Setup Time	Quick (minutes to hours)	Longer (days to weeks)
Compliance Requirements	Not suitable for strict needs	Ideal for regulated environments
Scalability	Limited by ISP bandwidth	Supports high-throughput workloads

Design Patterns for Hybrid Connectivity

There are various design patterns depending on business requirements:

- **VPN for Dev/Test, ExpressRoute for Production**: Cost-effective and strategic usage.

- **Failover Configuration**: Use VPN as a failover path for ExpressRoute.

- **Multi-Site Hybrid**: Connect multiple branches/offices to Azure with separate VPN tunnels or ER circuits.

- **Hub-and-Spoke**: On-prem connects to a central VNet, which then peers with multiple spoke VNets in Azure.

Best Practices for Hybrid Network Security and Performance

1. **Use BGP where possible**: For dynamic routing and improved failover support.

2. **Split tunneling carefully**: Prevent sending all traffic through Azure unless necessary.

3. **Deploy Azure Firewall or NVA in hub**: Enforce central policy management.

4. **Implement NSGs and route tables (UDRs)**: Ensure traffic is segmented and monitored.

5. **Enable diagnostics**: Use Network Watcher, Log Analytics, and Traffic Analytics.

6. **Regularly audit**: Validate connectivity, security posture, and cost metrics.

Monitoring and Troubleshooting Hybrid Connectivity

Use the following tools for operational excellence:

- **Azure Network Watcher**:
  - Connection Monitor
  - Topology Viewer
  - IP Flow Verify
  - Packet Capture

- **Log Analytics** and **Azure Monitor**: Aggregate performance and security logs.

Connectivity Tests:

```
az network watcher connection-monitor create \
  --name TestConnection \
```

```
--resource-group MyResourceGroup \
--location eastus \
--source-resource MyVM \
--dest-address www.bing.com \
--dest-port 80
```

•

VPN **Troubleshooting** **Commands**:

```
az network vpn-connection show \
  --name MyConnection \
  --resource-group MyResourceGroup
```

- Look for `connectionStatus` (should be `Connected`), and examine logs for `EgressBytesTransferred`, `IngressPacketsDropped`, etc.

Summary

Hybrid network architectures are essential for organizations bridging on-premises infrastructure and cloud-based environments. Azure provides two robust options—VPN and ExpressRoute—each suited to different needs, budgets, and performance expectations. Understanding the technical and operational differences between them allows architects to design networks that are scalable, resilient, and secure.

By leveraging Azure tools for automation, monitoring, and diagnostics, hybrid environments can be managed with agility and precision, ensuring a seamless extension of enterprise networks into the cloud.

DNS and Name Resolution Strategies

In any network—on-premises or cloud—Domain Name System (DNS) is a foundational component that enables applications, services, and users to resolve hostnames to IP addresses. In Azure hybrid environments, DNS becomes even more critical due to the presence of both on-premises and cloud resources that must seamlessly interact. This section explores Azure's DNS capabilities, how they integrate with traditional DNS infrastructure, and advanced name resolution strategies suitable for hybrid deployments.

Role of DNS in Hybrid Networks

DNS is more than just a convenience; it's essential for:

- Resource discovery (e.g., finding a storage account or database)
- Service availability and routing
- Security (e.g., via filtering malicious domains)
- Load distribution and redundancy

In hybrid networks, DNS must be capable of resolving:

- On-premises hostnames from Azure
- Azure hostnames from on-premises
- Private endpoints and service integrations
- External internet resources

Managing DNS in a hybrid architecture often involves bridging internal DNS zones, forwarding queries across network boundaries, and establishing secure, low-latency resolution paths.

DNS Options in Azure

Azure provides several DNS capabilities, each designed for specific use cases:

DNS Type	Description
Azure DNS (Public)	Public DNS service hosting internet-accessible DNS zones
Azure Private DNS Zones	Internal name resolution for resources in a virtual network
Custom DNS Servers	User-defined DNS servers configured at the VNet or NIC level
Azure-Provided DNS	Default DNS service available on every VNet (at 168.63.129.16)

Each of these can be leveraged and combined to achieve a secure and performant hybrid DNS architecture.

Azure-Provided DNS

By default, Azure VMs use a built-in DNS service that resides at the IP address `168.63.129.16`. This service automatically provides resolution for:

- Azure hostnames within the same VNet

- Basic internal name resolution across subnets

Limitations:

- Cannot resolve on-premises hostnames

- Cannot customize internal zones

- Not suitable for complex hybrid architectures

Custom DNS Servers in Azure

You can configure Azure virtual networks to use custom DNS servers—either running in Azure (e.g., Windows Server with DNS Role) or pointing to on-premises DNS servers over a VPN or ExpressRoute connection.

Configuring Custom DNS for a VNet

```
az network vnet update \
  --name MyVNet \
  --resource-group MyResourceGroup \
  --dns-servers 10.1.0.4 10.1.0.5
```

> These IP addresses can point to custom DNS VMs or an on-prem DNS server reachable via hybrid connectivity.

Custom DNS enables resolution of both cloud and on-prem names. However, it requires management of DNS infrastructure and replication of zones if needed.

Azure Private DNS Zones

Azure Private DNS Zones allow you to define custom domain names and resolve them privately within Azure VNets. This is ideal for hybrid scenarios where you want full control over DNS naming for internal services.

Key Features:

- VNet integration (auto-registration for VM hostnames)

- Split-horizon DNS (same domain, different resolution internally vs externally)

- Zone linking across VNets (even across regions)

Example: Creating and Linking a Private DNS Zone

```
# Create a private DNS zone
az network private-dns zone create \
  --resource-group MyResourceGroup \
  --name internal.contoso.com

# Link it to a VNet
az network private-dns link vnet create \
  --resource-group MyResourceGroup \
  --zone-name internal.contoso.com \
  --name MyDNSLink \
  --virtual-network MyVNet \
  --registration-enabled true
```

Hybrid DNS Forwarding Strategy

One of the biggest challenges in hybrid DNS is forwarding requests from Azure to on-premises and vice versa. This typically requires DNS forwarders that route queries to the appropriate resolver based on the domain namespace.

Pattern: Azure to On-Prem DNS Resolution

1. Azure VM sends query to custom DNS server (e.g., 10.1.0.4)

2. Custom DNS forwards queries for corp.contoso.com to on-premises DNS via VPN/ExpressRoute

3. On-prem DNS resolves the query and returns result

This setup requires DNS forwarding rules:

- On Azure DNS server:
  - Forward corp.contoso.com to on-prem DNS (e.g., 192.168.0.4)

- On-prem DNS:

  - Optionally forward `azure.local` or similar to Azure DNS forwarder

Deploying DNS Forwarder in Azure

You can deploy a DNS forwarder using a Windows Server VM or a Linux VM running `dnsmasq` or `bind9`.

Example (Windows DNS Forwarder Setup):

1. Install DNS role via Server Manager or PowerShell

2. Set forwarder for `corp.contoso.com` pointing to `192.168.0.4`

3. Enable conditional forwarding in the DNS Manager

Example (Linux dnsmasq):

```
sudo apt install dnsmasq
```

Add to `/etc/dnsmasq.conf`:

```
server=/corp.contoso.com/192.168.0.4
listen-address=10.1.0.4
```

Restart the service:

```
sudo systemctl restart dnsmasq
```

Split-Horizon DNS

Split-horizon DNS (also called split-view DNS) allows internal and external clients to resolve the same domain name to different IPs. Azure Private DNS Zones support this when used alongside public DNS.

Example:

- Public DNS (`app.contoso.com`) resolves to `52.123.4.56` (public IP)

- Private DNS (`app.contoso.com` in Azure Private DNS Zone) resolves to `10.1.2.4` (internal   IP)

When a request originates within Azure, the private resolution takes precedence.

Integrating with Active Directory

For organizations using **Active Directory Domain Services (AD DS)** or **Azure AD DS**, DNS integration is critical for domain-joined VMs and authentication workflows.

Scenarios:

- Domain   join   VMs   in   Azure   to   on-prem   AD   over   VPN

- Use   Azure   AD   DS   with   integrated   DNS   zone

- Conditional   forwarding   to   resolve   both   environments

Important Ports:

Ensure the following ports are open on the VPN/ExpressRoute:

- TCP/UDP   53   (DNS)

- TCP/UDP   389,   636   (LDAP/LDAPS)

- TCP   445   (SMB   for   GPOs)

High Availability and Security for DNS

DNS outages or vulnerabilities can take entire systems offline. In hybrid deployments:

- Deploy   multiple   DNS   servers   across   AZs   and   regions

- Use   NSGs   to   restrict   DNS   traffic

- Implement   DNS   logging   and   alerting   with   Azure   Monitor

- Secure   DNS   servers   from   external   exposure

Monitoring DNS Resolution in Azure

You can use **Azure Monitor**, **Network Watcher**, and custom logging to monitor DNS performance and troubleshoot failures.

Sample Diagnostic Setup for Private DNS Zone:

```
az monitor diagnostic-settings create \
  --resource                              "/subscriptions/<sub-
id>/resourceGroups/MyResourceGroup/providers/Microsoft.Network/priva
teDnsZones/internal.contoso.com" \
  --name dnsLogs \
  --workspace                             "/subscriptions/<sub-
id>/resourceGroups/MyResourceGroup/providers/Microsoft.OperationalIn
sights/workspaces/MyWorkspace" \
  --logs '[{"category": "AllMetrics", "enabled": true}]'
```

Common DNS Pitfalls in Hybrid Networks

1. **Circular   DNS   Forwarding**:

   ○ Avoid forwarding back and forth between on-prem and Azure DNS servers.

2. **Unreachable   DNS   Servers**:

   ○ Verify   connectivity   across   VPN/ExpressRoute;   use   diagnostics.

3. **Unlinked   Private   DNS   Zones**:

   ○ Zones   must   be   linked   to   VNets   for   resolution.

4. **DNS   Cache   Inconsistencies**:

   ○ Flush DNS when making changes: `ipconfig /flushdns` or `systemd-resolve                                --flush-caches`.

Summary

DNS in hybrid Azure environments requires careful planning to ensure name resolution across diverse infrastructure. Azure provides flexible tools like private DNS zones, custom DNS servers, and integrations with on-prem environments to enable reliable DNS resolution.

A well-architected DNS strategy ensures:

- Seamless hybrid communication
- Secure and audited resolution paths
- High availability and redundancy
- Support for split-horizon configurations

In the next section, we'll explore how to manage traffic flow in these hybrid networks using routing, firewalls, and load balancing components.

Managing Traffic Flow in Hybrid Environments

Traffic management in hybrid cloud environments is a sophisticated but vital aspect of maintaining performance, security, and availability. When applications, users, and services span on-premises data centers and Azure, controlling how traffic flows between these locations becomes critical. Without a robust traffic management strategy, you risk bottlenecks, inefficient routing, security vulnerabilities, and poor user experience.

This section explores routing methods, network segmentation, traffic filtering, load balancing, and optimization strategies to effectively manage traffic flow in a hybrid Azure setup. You'll learn how to direct traffic between networks intelligently, minimize latency, and enforce security and governance policies.

Goals of Hybrid Traffic Management

An effective traffic management strategy in hybrid environments aims to:

- Ensure **efficient routing** between on-premises and cloud
- Maintain **high availability** through failover and redundancy
- Enforce **security policies** through segmentation and filtering
- Optimize for **performance** and **latency**
- Provide **observability** for monitoring and troubleshooting

Meeting these goals requires understanding and leveraging several Azure-native and custom mechanisms.

Azure Routing Basics

Azure uses **System Routes** and **User-Defined Routes (UDRs)** to control traffic. In a hybrid environment, these determine how traffic is sent to and from on-premises networks.

System Routes

These are default routes automatically created by Azure:

- VNet-to-VNet: Automatically knows how to route between subnets and peered VNets

- Internet: Routes 0.0.0.0/0 to the internet

- Hybrid: Routes traffic through the VPN Gateway or ExpressRoute gateway

You can inspect system routes:

```
az network nic show-effective-route-table \
  --name MyVMNic \
  --resource-group MyResourceGroup
```

User-Defined Routes (UDRs)

UDRs override system routes and are used to:

- Direct traffic through a network virtual appliance (NVA) or firewall

- Bypass default internet routing

- Customize hybrid traffic paths

Example: Route all on-prem traffic to the Azure Firewall

```
az network route-table create \
  --name MyRouteTable \
  --resource-group MyResourceGroup \
  --location eastus

az network route-table route create \
  --resource-group MyResourceGroup \
  --route-table-name MyRouteTable \
  --name OnPremTraffic \
  --address-prefix 192.168.0.0/16 \
  --next-hop-type VirtualAppliance \
```

```
--next-hop-ip-address 10.1.0.4
```

Attach the route table to a subnet:

```
az network vnet subnet update \
  --vnet-name MyVNet \
  --name MySubnet \
  --resource-group MyResourceGroup \
  --route-table MyRouteTable
```

Peering and Traffic Control Between VNets

In hybrid networks, traffic often flows between multiple VNets that are either peered or connected through a hub-and-spoke topology.

VNet Peering

- Low-latency, high-bandwidth connection between VNets

- Uses the Azure backbone; no gateway needed

- Traffic stays private

Traffic between peered VNets follows system routes unless overridden by UDRs. Peering can be configured with or without **forwarded traffic** and **gateway transit**, which are essential in hybrid setups.

Example: Enabling Gateway Transit

When connecting a spoke VNet to an on-prem network via a hub:

```
az network vnet peering create \
  --name SpokeToHub \
  --resource-group MyResourceGroup \
  --vnet-name SpokeVNet \
  --remote-vnet HubVNet \
  --allow-vnet-access \
  --allow-forwarded-traffic \
  --use-remote-gateways ,
```

Traffic Segmentation with NSGs and Route Tables

To enforce control and visibility, segment your traffic using **Network Security Groups (NSGs)** and strategic subnetting.

NSGs Example:

Allow only HTTP traffic to a web tier subnet:

```
az network nsg rule create \
  --resource-group MyResourceGroup \
  --nsg-name WebNSG \
  --name AllowHTTP \
  --protocol Tcp \
  --direction Inbound \
  --priority 100 \
  --source-address-prefixes '*' \
  --source-port-ranges '*' \
  --destination-address-prefixes '*' \
  --destination-port-ranges 80 \
  --access Allow
```

Block all other traffic by default or with lower-priority rules. NSGs are crucial to limit what can traverse subnets, particularly in hub-and-spoke architectures.

Azure Firewall and NVAs

Routing traffic through a centralized firewall (Azure Firewall or NVA like Palo Alto, Fortinet, etc.) enhances control and inspection.

Use Case: Force Tunneling via Azure Firewall

Force tunneling sends all outbound traffic—including internet-bound traffic—from Azure resources to the on-prem firewall or a cloud-based firewall for inspection.

- Create UDRs with 0.0.0.0/0 pointing to the firewall
- Enable **Forced Tunneling** in the VPN/ER gateway config
- Set up return routes accordingly

Azure Firewall Example:

```
az network firewall create \
  --name MyAzureFirewall \
  --resource-group MyResourceGroup \
```

```
  --location eastus

az network firewall network-rule create \
  --firewall-name MyAzureFirewall \
  --resource-group MyResourceGroup \
  --collection-name AllowWebTraffic \
  --name AllowHTTP \
  --rule-type NetworkRule \
  --priority 100 \
  --action Allow \
  --protocols TCP \
  --source-addresses 10.1.0.0/16 \
  --destination-addresses 0.0.0.0/0 \
  --destination-ports 80
```

Load Balancing Across Hybrid Deployments

Hybrid deployments may involve load balancing between on-prem and cloud instances or across multiple Azure regions.

Azure Load Balancer

- Layer 4 (TCP/UDP)

- Distributes traffic within Azure only

Azure Application Gateway

- Layer 7 (HTTP/HTTPS)

- Provides URL-based routing and WAF capabilities

- Works well with hybrid APIs and web apps

Azure Traffic Manager

- DNS-based global routing

- Ideal for hybrid-active or failover routing between on-prem and cloud

Example: Priority-based failover setup

```
az network traffic-manager profile create \
  --name HybridProfile \
  --resource-group MyResourceGroup \
  --routing-method Priority \
  --unique-dns-name myhybridapp \
  --ttl 30 \
  --monitor-path / \
  --monitor-port 80 \
  --monitor-protocol HTTP
```

Add endpoints for on-prem and Azure web apps, setting Azure as secondary.

Bandwidth Management and Throttling

Hybrid connectivity over VPN/ExpressRoute has finite bandwidth. Use throttling and QoS policies to prioritize traffic:

- Use **Azure QoS policies** to prioritize business-critical apps

- Segment traffic flows using **custom UDRs**

- Monitor with **Network Performance Monitor** and **Log Analytics**

Observability and Troubleshooting

Azure provides tools to gain visibility into how traffic flows and where issues arise.

Tools:

- **Network Watcher:**

  - Topology Viewer

  - IP Flow Verify

  - Connection Monitor

- **Log Analytics:**

  - Logs from Azure Firewall, NSGs, VPN Gateway

- **Traffic** **Analytics:**

  - Visual flow analysis and hotspot detection

Example: IP Flow Verification

```
az network watcher ip-flow-verify \
  --resource-group MyResourceGroup \
  --location eastus \
  --direction Inbound \
  --protocol TCP \
  --local 10.1.2.4 \
  --remote 203.0.113.1 \
  --local-port 80 \
  --remote-port 50000 \
  --nic-id /subscriptions/.../networkInterfaces/MyNic
```

Design Patterns for Hybrid Traffic

1. **Hub-and-Spoke with Centralized Firewall**
   Traffic flows through a hub VNet where inspection and routing occur.

2. **Direct Spoke-to-On-Prem Routes**
   Each spoke has direct VPN connections for low latency but increases complexity.

3. **Active/Passive or Active/Active Failover**
   Use Traffic Manager or custom scripts for resilience.

4. **Split Routing Based on Traffic Type**
   Use UDRs to route different types of traffic (e.g., corporate vs. internet-bound) via different gateways.

Security Considerations

- **Zero Trust Networking**: Never trust by default; enforce identity and conditional access.

- **Least Privilege Routing**: Only allow routes that are necessary.

- **Audit All Traffic Paths**: Use Azure Policy and Diagnostic Logs to track route configurations.

- **Encryption In Transit**: Ensure IPsec VPNs or ExpressRoute encryption is enabled.

- **NVA Hardening**: Apply security updates and restrict management access.

Summary

Managing traffic flow in hybrid environments is a balancing act of performance, control, and security. Azure equips you with flexible tools—routing tables, peering, firewalls, and load balancers—to build intelligent network paths tailored to your architecture.

By applying proper segmentation, centralized routing, observability tools, and redundancy, your hybrid network can meet enterprise-grade performance and security expectations. This careful planning and control ensure your cloud journey is smooth, secure, and future-proof.

Next, we'll dive into the tools and methodologies for **monitoring and troubleshooting** hybrid networks to ensure ongoing reliability.

Monitoring and Troubleshooting Hybrid Networks

Monitoring and troubleshooting hybrid networks in Azure is essential for ensuring uptime, performance, security, and compliance. Hybrid environments introduce additional complexity due to the involvement of on-premises networks, VPN or ExpressRoute connections, Azure VNets, and multiple routing and security layers.

This section provides comprehensive strategies, tools, and techniques to effectively monitor, diagnose, and resolve issues across your hybrid networking infrastructure. We'll cover everything from real-time visibility to proactive alerting and reactive troubleshooting, using Azure-native services and best practices.

Objectives of Hybrid Network Monitoring

An effective monitoring strategy should:

- Provide **end-to-end** **visibility** across on-prem and cloud resources

- Detect and diagnose **connectivity** **issues**

- Track **latency,** **packet** **loss,** **and** **throughput**

- Ensure **security** **compliance** and alert on anomalies

- Offer historical **trend** **analysis** and **capacity** **planning**

- Enable **automated** **response** or escalation mechanisms

Monitoring should span all layers: physical connections, routing, DNS, firewalling, and application-level performance.

Key Azure Monitoring Tools

1. Azure Monitor

Azure Monitor is a unified platform for collecting, analyzing, and acting on telemetry from Azure and on-premises resources.

- Supports metrics, logs, and alerts

- Integrates with Log Analytics for custom queries

- Provides Workbooks for dashboarding

2. Network Watcher

Purpose-built for network monitoring and diagnostics in Azure:

- Connection Monitor

- Topology Viewer

- IP Flow Verify

- Packet Capture

- Next Hop

- NSG Flow Logs

3. Azure Log Analytics

A powerful query engine for analyzing logs from:

- NSGs

- VPN   Gateways

- ExpressRoute

- Firewalls

- Application   Gateways

4. Azure Traffic Analytics

Builds on NSG Flow Logs to provide heatmaps, traffic patterns, and threat detection.

5. Network Performance Monitor (NPM)

Part of Azure Monitor; allows end-to-end performance monitoring between Azure and on-prem environments using agents.

Setting Up Diagnostics

Enable NSG Flow Logs

NSG Flow Logs capture network traffic metadata (source, destination, ports, etc.).

```
az network watcher flow-log configure \
  --resource-group MyResourceGroup \
  --nsg MyNSG \
  --enabled true \
  --storage-account MyStorageAccount \
  --retention 30 \
  --log-version 2
```

Optional: Integrate with Traffic Analytics

```
az network watcher flow-log configure \
  --resource-group MyResourceGroup \
  --nsg MyNSG \
  --traffic-analytics true \
  --workspace MyLogAnalyticsWorkspace
```

Enable VPN Diagnostics

```
az network watcher diagnostic-settings create \
```

```
  --resource                                    /subscriptions/<sub-
id>/resourceGroups/MyRG/providers/Microsoft.Network/connections/MyVP
NConnection \
  --workspace MyLogAnalyticsWorkspace \
  --name VPNDiagnostics \
  --logs '[{"category": "TunnelDiagnosticLog", "enabled": true}]'
```

Enable ExpressRoute Monitoring

ExpressRoute supports metrics like bytes sent/received, route changes, and BGP peering status.

```
az monitor metrics list \
  --resource                                    /subscriptions/<sub-
id>/resourceGroups/MyRG/providers/Microsoft.Network/expressRouteCirc
uits/MyCircuit \
  --metric-names "BitsInPerSecond" "BitsOutPerSecond"
```

Use alerts to notify teams of drops or abnormal values.

Connection Monitor

Connection Monitor tests connectivity between Azure resources and external or on-prem endpoints, simulating real user paths.

Create a Connection Monitor

```
az network watcher connection-monitor create \
  --name HybridConnMon \
  --resource-group MyResourceGroup \
  --location eastus \
  --source-resource MyVM \
  --dest-address 10.0.0.10 \
  --dest-port 443
```

Use this to test:

- VNet   to   VNet   connections
- Azure   to   on-prem

- Azure to internet destinations

Visualize latency, jitter, and packet loss over time.

Troubleshooting Scenarios

Scenario 1: VPN Tunnel Not Connecting

Symptoms:

- VPN connection shows "Disconnected"
- Resources can't reach on-prem services

Steps:

1. Validate shared key and IPs in `az network vpn-connection show`
2. Use Connection Monitor to test path
3. Check local firewall and NSGs blocking ports (UDP 500, UDP 4500)
4. Run packet capture:

```
az network watcher packet-capture create \
  --name VPNTroubleshoot \
  --resource-group MyResourceGroup \
  --vm-name MyVPNVM \
  --storage-account MyStorageAccount \
  --filters '[{"protocol": "UDP", "localPort": "500"}]'
```

5. Validate routes in `az network nic show-effective-route-table`

Scenario 2: DNS Resolution Fails

Symptoms:

- VMs cannot resolve on-prem hostnames

- Applications time out

Steps:

1. Verify custom DNS settings on VNet/subnet level
2. Ensure DNS forwarders can reach on-prem DNS via VPN
3. Use `nslookup` from VM:

```
nslookup myapp.corp.contoso.com 10.1.0.4
```

4. Check for DNS loop or lack of forwarding rules
5. Enable DNS query logging on the forwarder VM

Scenario 3: Application Latency Between Azure and On-Prem

Symptoms:

- Azure-hosted services respond slowly to on-prem requests

Steps:

1. Run Connection Monitor with latency tracking
2. Check ExpressRoute metrics (jitter, bandwidth)
3. Use Log Analytics to query App Gateway logs:

```
AzureDiagnostics
| where ResourceType == "APPLICATIONGATEWAYS"
| summarize avg(DurationMs) by bin(TimeGenerated, 5m)
```

4. Review NSG flow logs for packet drops or retransmissions
5. Inspect routes—ensure traffic isn't hairpinning through unnecessary paths

---

Scenario 4: Failover Not Triggering

Symptoms:

- ExpressRoute down, but VPN not taking over

Steps:

1. Check routing priorities and weights

2. Use "Next Hop" tool:

```
az network watcher next-hop \
  --resource-group MyResourceGroup \
  --vm-name MyVM \
  --destination-ip 192.168.1.4
```

3. Confirm UDRs don't force all traffic to a downed appliance

4. Monitor BGP state:

```
az network express-route peering list \
  --resource-group MyRG \
  --circuit-name MyCircuit
```

5. Ensure connection weights on VPN and ExpressRoute are set correctly in the route table

---

Alerting and Automation

Proactive alerting helps you catch issues before users are affected.

Sample Alert Rule: High Latency

```
az monitor metrics alert create \
  --name HighLatencyAlert \
  --resource-group MyResourceGroup \
  --scopes                        "/subscriptions/<sub-
id>/resourceGroups/MyRG/providers/Microsoft.Network/connectionMonito
rs/HybridConnMon" \
```

```
--condition "avg roundTripTime > 200" \
--description "Alert when hybrid link latency > 200ms" \
--action-groups MyActionGroup
```

Other useful alert conditions:

- VPN tunnel down
- High packet loss
- Dropped packets in NSG logs
- DNS resolution failures

Automation ideas:

- Restart VPN Gateway
- Redeploy connection monitor
- Auto-ticket creation via Logic Apps

Best Practices

1. **Centralize Logging**: Use a single Log Analytics Workspace.
2. **Tag Resources**: Easier to filter logs and metrics.
3. **Use Workbooks**: Create visual dashboards for traffic, connectivity, latency.
4. **Baseline Performance**: Know what "normal" looks like to detect anomalies.
5. **Monitor Both Ends**: On-prem and Azure agents for complete visibility.
6. **Document Runbooks**: For incident response and escalation procedures.

Summary

Monitoring and troubleshooting hybrid networks in Azure requires a layered approach that combines real-time telemetry, historical analytics, intelligent alerting, and deep diagnostics.

With tools like Network Watcher, Log Analytics, and Connection Monitor, Azure provides rich insights into hybrid connectivity.

By adopting proactive practices—such as enabling diagnostics, setting thresholds, and integrating with automation—you can maintain a resilient hybrid infrastructure that scales and adapts to business needs. Proper observability not only helps resolve incidents quickly but also enables optimization and growth of your network footprint.

In the next chapter, we'll move beyond hybrid networking and explore advanced Azure networking components like Application Gateways, Traffic Manager, and Private Link.

Chapter 5: Advanced Networking Components

Azure Load Balancers and Traffic Manager

Modern applications require high availability, scalability, and low latency. To meet these requirements, Azure provides powerful load distribution tools—**Azure Load Balancer** and **Azure Traffic Manager**—that help ensure your application remains available and responsive, whether deployed in a single region or across the globe.

This section will dive deep into the architecture, use cases, configuration, and optimization techniques for both solutions. We'll also explore the differences between the two, discuss when to use one over the other (or both), and show how they can be integrated into larger networking strategies within hybrid and cloud-native architectures.

Understanding Load Balancing in Azure

Azure offers multiple options for distributing traffic depending on the OSI layer, traffic type, and application design:

Service	Layer	Scope	Protocols	Use Case
Azure Load Balancer	L4	Regional	TCP/UDP	Intra-region traffic, VM balancing
Traffic Manager	DNS	Global	Any (via DNS)	Global traffic routing
Application Gateway	L7	Regional	HTTP/HTTPS	Web traffic with WAF and routing

This section will focus on Azure Load Balancer and Traffic Manager. Application Gateway will be covered in the next section.

Azure Load Balancer

Azure Load Balancer is a Layer 4 (transport layer) load balancing solution that supports TCP and UDP traffic. It operates at the virtual network level and can distribute traffic across virtual machines, availability sets, or virtual machine scale sets (VMSS).

There are two main SKUs:

- **Basic Load Balancer** – Supports only a single availability set or VM set, lacks diagnostics

- **Standard Load Balancer** – Recommended for production, supports availability zones, diagnostics, and larger scale

Key Features:

- Inbound and outbound NAT

- High availability within a region

- Supports IPv4 and IPv6

- Integrated with Azure Monitor

- Supports HA ports (for NVA scenarios)

Internal vs Public Load Balancer

- **Public Load Balancer**: Exposes services to the internet using a public IP

- **Internal Load Balancer (ILB)**: Used for private communication within a virtual network or between peered VNets

---

Creating a Standard Load Balancer

Step 1: Create a Public IP Address

```
az network public-ip create \
  --name MyPublicIP \
  --resource-group MyResourceGroup \
  --sku Standard \
  --allocation-method static
```

Step 2: Create the Load Balancer

```
az network lb create \
  --resource-group MyResourceGroup \
  --name MyLoadBalancer \
```

```
--sku Standard \
--frontend-ip-name MyFrontEnd \
--backend-pool-name MyBackEndPool \
--public-ip-address MyPublicIP
```

Step 3: Define Health Probe

```
az network lb probe create \
  --resource-group MyResourceGroup \
  --lb-name MyLoadBalancer \
  --name MyHealthProbe \
  --protocol tcp \
  --port 80
```

Step 4: Add Load Balancing Rule

```
az network lb rule create \
  --resource-group MyResourceGroup \
  --lb-name MyLoadBalancer \
  --name HTTPRule \
  --protocol tcp \
  --frontend-port 80 \
  --backend-port 80 \
  --frontend-ip-name MyFrontEnd \
  --backend-pool-name MyBackEndPool \
  --probe-name MyHealthProbe
```

Step 5: Add VMs to Backend Pool

VMs must have their NICs associated with the backend pool:

```
az network nic ip-config address-pool add \
  --address-pool MyBackEndPool \
  --ip-config-name ipconfig1 \
  --nic-name MyVMNic \
  --resource-group MyResourceGroup \
  --lb-name MyLoadBalancer
```

Advanced Load Balancer Use Cases

1. Highly Available Web Tier

- Distribute requests across multiple VMs or scale sets

- Combine with App Gateway for L7 inspection

2. Network Virtual Appliance (NVA) Load Balancing

- Use HA ports to forward all traffic to a firewall/NVA

- Route all outbound/inbound traffic through the appliance

3. Multi-zone Load Balancing

- Use Standard SKU for support across Availability Zones

- Ensures fault tolerance across physical datacenters

4. Outbound Connections via Load Balancer

- Azure Standard Load Balancer enables SNAT (Source NAT) for outbound connections

---

Monitoring and Troubleshooting Load Balancer

Enable resource diagnostics and monitor health probes using:

```
az monitor diagnostic-settings create \
  --resource
/subscriptions/<id>/resourceGroups/MyResourceGroup/providers/Microso
ft.Network/loadBalancers/MyLoadBalancer \
  --workspace MyLogAnalyticsWorkspace \
  --name LBMonitor \
  --logs '[{"category": "LoadBalancerAlertEvent", "enabled": true}]'
```

Inspect load balancer metrics:

- DipAvailability

- ByteCount

- `PacketCount`

- `SnatConnectionCount`

Use `Connection Monitor` to validate end-to-end paths.

Azure Traffic Manager

Azure Traffic Manager is a global DNS-based traffic distribution solution. It routes incoming requests to the nearest or most appropriate endpoint based on configurable routing methods.

It does **not** serve as a proxy. Instead, it resolves to the best endpoint IP, after which clients connect directly.

Routing Methods:

Method	Description
Priority	Failover model: traffic flows to primary until failure, then to backup
Weighted	Percentage-based routing (A/B testing)
Performance	Lowest-latency endpoint based on DNS location
Geographic	Route based on client geographic location
Multivalue	Returns multiple healthy endpoints for redundancy
Subnet	Routes traffic based on user IP subnet

Creating a Traffic Manager Profile

Step 1: Create the Profile

```
az network traffic-manager profile create \
  --name MyTMProfile \
  --resource-group MyResourceGroup \
  --routing-method Performance \
  --unique-dns-name myapp-tm \
  --ttl 30 \
```

```
--monitor-path "/" \
--monitor-port 80 \
--monitor-protocol HTTP
```

Step 2: Add Endpoints

You can add Azure endpoints or external (non-Azure) endpoints:

```
az network traffic-manager endpoint create \
  --resource-group MyResourceGroup \
  --profile-name MyTMProfile \
  --type azureEndpoints \
  --name EastUSWebApp \
  --target-resource-id
/subscriptions/<id>/resourceGroups/rg1/providers/Microsoft.Network/p
ublicIPAddresses/webappIP \
  --endpoint-status Enabled
```

For on-prem or external websites:

```
az network traffic-manager endpoint create \
  --resource-group MyResourceGroup \
  --profile-name MyTMProfile \
  --type externalEndpoints \
  --name OnPremApp \
  --target "onprem.contoso.com" \
  --endpoint-status Enabled
```

Combining Load Balancer and Traffic Manager

A common enterprise pattern is to use both services together:

- **Traffic Manager** routes global DNS traffic across regions or endpoints

- **Load Balancer** handles regional distribution within each endpoint

Example Architecture:

- Client resolves app.contoso.com via Traffic Manager to East US endpoint

- East US Load Balancer distributes traffic among VMs in East US

- Health probes detect failures at both DNS and TCP level

This allows regional failover with intra-region high availability.

Traffic Manager Scenarios

1. Global Web App Failover

- Route users to nearest region with fallback to secondary

- Use Performance or Priority routing

2. Hybrid Workload Distribution

- Route traffic between Azure and on-prem based on weights or geography

3. Disaster Recovery Planning

- Use Priority routing for DR site readiness testing

4. Compliance and Data Sovereignty

- Use Geographic routing to ensure data remains in region (e.g., EU-only)

Monitoring Traffic Manager

Traffic Manager exposes health metrics and logs:

```
az monitor metrics list \
  --resource                              /subscriptions/<sub-
id>/resourceGroups/MyRG/providers/Microsoft.Network/trafficManagerPr
ofiles/MyTMProfile \
  --metric-names EndpointStatusByProfileResourceId
```

Health checks are based on HTTP/HTTPS/TCP probe results. Failed probes remove endpoint from rotation.

Alerts can be configured on:

- Endpoint   unavailability

- Traffic   pattern   anomalies

- High   DNS   resolution   failure   rate

Best Practices for Load Balancing and Traffic Management

1. **Use Standard SKU** for all new Load Balancer deployments for advanced features and diagnostics

2. **Set consistent health probes** across endpoints

3. **Leverage Availability Zones** for regional resilience

4. **Implement UDRs carefully** when using internal load balancers

5. **Validate DNS TTL settings** to control traffic redirection frequency

6. **Use ARM templates or Bicep** for repeatable deployment of configurations

7. **Monitor aggressively** with Azure Monitor and custom alerts

Summary

Azure Load Balancer and Traffic Manager are powerful and complementary tools that together form the backbone of modern, scalable, and resilient cloud networking solutions.

- Use **Load Balancer** for local/regional distribution of TCP/UDP traffic

- Use **Traffic Manager** for global routing and DNS-based decision-making

By combining both services, you can build applications that scale seamlessly, recover from failures gracefully, and provide an optimal experience for users around the world. These services are critical for any Azure solution operating at scale or spanning multiple regions and infrastructures.

In the next section, we will explore **Application Gateway** and **Web Application Firewall (WAF)** for deeper control and security at the HTTP layer.

Application Gateway and Web Application Firewall (WAF)

Azure Application Gateway is a Layer 7 load balancer with advanced traffic management capabilities, designed to handle web traffic. Unlike Azure Load Balancer, which operates at the transport layer, Application Gateway allows for routing decisions based on HTTP attributes such as URI path or host headers. It also provides a built-in **Web Application Firewall (WAF)** to protect applications against common threats such as SQL injection, cross-site scripting (XSS), and OWASP Top 10 vulnerabilities.

This section delves into the configuration, advanced features, use cases, and deployment scenarios of Azure Application Gateway with WAF, focusing on how it plays a vital role in modern cloud-native and hybrid application architectures.

Overview of Azure Application Gateway

Application Gateway is a fully managed service that provides application-level routing and protection. Key capabilities include:

- HTTP/HTTPS   traffic   routing

- URL-based   routing

- Host-based   routing

- SSL   termination   and   end-to-end   SSL

- Cookie-based   session   affinity

- Custom   probes

- Autoscaling

- Web   Application   Firewall   (WAF)   integration

The Application Gateway is ideal for modern web workloads that require intelligent routing, multi-site hosting, and layered security.

Key Components

Component	Description

Frontend IP   The public or private IP that receives client requests

Listener   Listens for incoming connections on a specific protocol/port

Backend Pool   Set of resources (VMs, App Services, IPs) receiving routed traffic

Rules   Define how requests are routed based on conditions

HTTP Settings   Port, protocol, affinity, probe settings for backend communication

WAF Policy   Security rules to inspect and block malicious traffic

Deployment Options

You can deploy Application Gateway in two main modes:

- **Standard/Standard_v2** – Basic L7 load balancing, no WAF

- **WAF/WAF_v2** – Includes the Web Application Firewall functionality

The v2 SKU offers better performance, autoscaling, and zone redundancy.

Use Cases

1. **Multi-site Hosting** – Host multiple domains behind a single gateway with host-based routing

2. **SSL Termination and Re-encryption** – Offload SSL from backend servers, with optional re-encryption

3. **Web Application Protection** – Use WAF to secure apps from malicious inputs and known vulnerabilities

4. **Session Affinity** – Sticky sessions based on cookies for stateful web applications

5. **Custom Health Probes** – Determine app health beyond TCP connectivity

Creating an Application Gateway with WAF

Step 1: Create Public IP

```
az network public-ip create \
  --resource-group MyResourceGroup \
  --name MyAGPublicIP \
  --sku Standard \
  --allocation-method Static
```

Step 2: Create Virtual Network

```
az network vnet create \
  --name MyVNet \
  --resource-group MyResourceGroup \
  --location eastus \
  --address-prefix 10.0.0.0/16 \
  --subnet-name AppGatewaySubnet \
  --subnet-prefix 10.0.1.0/24
```

> Note: The subnet name must be AppGatewaySubnet or named specifically for Application Gateway use.

Step 3: Create Application Gateway

```
az network application-gateway create \
  --name MyAppGateway \
  --location eastus \
  --resource-group MyResourceGroup \
  --capacity 2 \
  --sku WAF_v2 \
  --frontend-port 80 \
  --http-settings-cookie-based-affinity Enabled \
  --vnet-name MyVNet \
  --subnet AppGatewaySubnet \
  --public-ip-address MyAGPublicIP
```

You can further customize it with HTTPS support, backend pools, listeners, and routing rules.

Configuring Listeners and Rules

Add a new HTTP listener

```
az network application-gateway http-listener create \
  --resource-group MyResourceGroup \
  --gateway-name MyAppGateway \
  --name MyListener \
  --frontend-port 80 \
  --frontend-ip MyFrontEndIP \
  --protocol Http
```

Create a rule for routing

```
az network application-gateway rule create \
  --resource-group MyResourceGroup \
  --gateway-name MyAppGateway \
  --name MyRoutingRule \
  --http-listener MyListener \
  --rule-type Basic \
  --http-settings MyHTTPSettings \
  --backend-pool MyBackEndPool
```

URL Path-Based Routing

Azure Application Gateway allows URL path routing, which is ideal for microservices or segmented application layers.

Example:

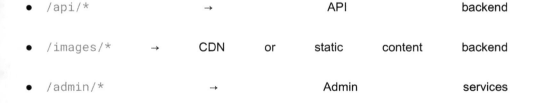

- `/api/*` → API backend

- `/images/*` → CDN or static content backend

- `/admin/*` → Admin services

```
az network application-gateway url-path-map create \
  --resource-group MyResourceGroup \
  --gateway-name MyAppGateway \
  --name MyPathMap \
  --default-backend-address-pool MyBackEndPool \
  --default-http-settings MyHTTPSettings
```

```
az network application-gateway url-path-map rule create \
  --resource-group MyResourceGroup \
  --gateway-name MyAppGateway \
  --path-map-name MyPathMap \
  --name APIRoute \
  --paths /api/* \
  --backend-address-pool APIBackEndPool \
  --http-settings APIHTTPSettings
```

Enabling and Configuring WAF

WAF inspects all incoming HTTP(S) traffic and blocks requests that match attack patterns defined in the OWASP core rule sets (CRS).·

Enabling WAF Mode

WAF has two operational modes:

- **Detection** – Logs but does not block malicious requests

- **Prevention** – Blocks malicious traffic

```
az network application-gateway waf-config set \
  --enabled true \
  --gateway-name MyAppGateway \
  --resource-group MyResourceGroup \
  --firewall-mode Prevention \
  --rule-set-type OWASP \
  --rule-set-version 3.2
```

Custom WAF Rules

Create rules to allow/block traffic based on IP, region, headers, etc.

```
az network application-gateway waf-policy custom-rule create \
  --policy-name MyWAFPolicy \
  --resource-group MyResourceGroup \
  --name BlockMaliciousIPs \
  --priority 100 \
  --rule-type MatchRule \
```

```
  --action Block \
  --match-conditions     match-variables=RemoteAddr     operator=IPMatch
values=192.168.1.10
```

Attach the WAF policy to the Application Gateway:

```
az network application-gateway waf-policy set \
  --gateway-name MyAppGateway \
  --resource-group MyResourceGroup \
  --policy-name MyWAFPolicy
```

Monitoring Application Gateway

Application Gateway exposes rich telemetry:

- **Access Logs** – Information about incoming requests
- **Performance Logs** – Latency and throughput metrics
- **Firewall Logs** – WAF hits and blocks

Enable Diagnostic Settings

```
az monitor diagnostic-settings create \
  --resource                           "/subscriptions/<sub-
id>/resourceGroups/MyResourceGroup/providers/Microsoft.Network/appli
cationGateways/MyAppGateway" \
  --workspace MyLogAnalyticsWorkspace \
  --name AGMonitor \
  --logs '[{"category": "ApplicationGatewayAccessLog", "enabled":
true}]'
```

You can visualize this data in Azure Monitor Workbooks or query it in Log Analytics:

```
AzureDiagnostics
| where ResourceType == "APPLICATIONGATEWAYS"
| summarize count() by httpStatus_d, bin(TimeGenerated, 5m)
```

Application Gateway in Hybrid Architectures

In hybrid networks, Application Gateway acts as a bridge between external clients and on-prem resources securely published through Azure. Common hybrid setups include:

- **Publishing On-Prem Web Apps** using Azure Application Gateway with **VPN or ExpressRoute**

- **Secure Reverse Proxy** with WAF protecting internal services

- **SSL Offloading** for on-prem applications using frontend termination in Azure

Traffic flows:

1. Client connects to public IP of Application Gateway

2. WAF inspects and routes based on rules

3. Request is forwarded to backend over private link, VPN, or ExpressRoute

---

Best Practices

1. **Use WAF_v2 SKU** for modern features and autoscaling

2. **Enable WAF in Prevention Mode** for production workloads

3. **Create separate pools and settings** for each logical backend

4. **Use SSL Termination** to simplify certificate management

5. **Leverage Path-Based Routing** for clean architecture

6. **Use health probes** that match real application behavior

7. **Use Application Gateway behind Azure Front Door** for global load balancing

8. **Automate deployment** using ARM/Bicep/Terraform templates

---

Summary

Azure Application Gateway with WAF is a robust and feature-rich solution for secure, scalable, and intelligent traffic management at the application layer. It empowers developers and network engineers to fine-tune request routing, protect web applications, and build modern microservices architectures.

With URL-based routing, SSL offload, session affinity, and deep integration with Azure services, Application Gateway is an essential component in cloud-native and hybrid deployments. When combined with Azure Load Balancer and Traffic Manager, it provides end-to-end control from global DNS-based distribution to secure, path-aware routing at the regional level.

In the next section, we will explore **Private Link and Private Endpoints**, which offer secure and private connectivity to Azure services without traversing the public internet.

Private Link and Private Endpoints

Azure Private Link and Private Endpoints enable secure, private access to Azure services and customer-owned services. These services provide network isolation and eliminate exposure to the public internet, making them ideal for organizations with strict security, compliance, or data sovereignty requirements.

Private Link ensures that traffic between a virtual network and Azure services remains entirely on the Microsoft backbone, providing a more secure and lower-latency communication path. This section explores how Private Link and Private Endpoints work, how to configure them, and how they integrate with hybrid and enterprise networking strategies.

Understanding Private Link and Private Endpoints

Private Link enables access to Azure services over a private IP in your virtual network. It abstracts the concept of Private Endpoints and Private Link Services under a unified approach to private connectivity.

Private Endpoint is a network interface with a private IP address that connects your VNet to a Private Link resource. It brings the service into your virtual network.

Private Link Service is used to expose your own services privately to other VNets, even from other tenants.

Key Benefits

- **Eliminates exposure to public internet**
- **Improves security and compliance posture**
- **Integrates with NSGs, UDRs, and Azure Firewall**
- **Supports many Azure PaaS services** (Storage, SQL, Cosmos DB, Key Vault, etc.)

- **Works across regions and subscriptions**

Supported Services

Some common services that support Private Endpoint connections:

- Azure Storage
- Azure SQL Database
- Azure Cosmos DB
- Azure Key Vault
- Azure App Services (Web Apps)
- Azure Kubernetes Service (AKS)
- Azure Web PubSub
- Azure Container Registry

You can also create **Private Link Services** to expose your custom workloads.

How It Works

1. A **Private Endpoint** is created in your VNet.
2. Azure assigns a **private IP** to the endpoint.
3. DNS configuration is updated to resolve service FQDNs to the private IP.
4. Traffic to the service is routed through the private link.

This ensures that even when using public service URLs, the traffic remains within the private network.

Example: Creating a Private Endpoint for Azure Storage

Step 1: Create a Virtual Network

```
az network vnet create \
  --resource-group MyResourceGroup \
  --name MyVNet \
  --address-prefix 10.0.0.0/16 \
  --subnet-name MySubnet \
  --subnet-prefix 10.0.1.0/24
```

Step 2: Create a Storage Account

```
az storage account create \
  --name mystorageacct2025 \
  --resource-group MyResourceGroup \
  --location eastus \
  --sku Standard_LRS \
  --kind StorageV2
```

Step 3: Create the Private Endpoint

```
az network private-endpoint create \
  --name MyPrivateEndpoint \
  --resource-group MyResourceGroup \
  --vnet-name MyVNet \
  --subnet MySubnet \
  --private-connection-resource-id $(az storage account show --name
mystorageacct2025 --query 'id' -o tsv) \
  --group-id blob \
  --connection-name StoragePrivateConnection
```

Step 4: Configure DNS (Manually or Automatically)

Private DNS Zone for blob storage:

```
az network private-dns zone create \
  --resource-group MyResourceGroup \
  --name "privatelink.blob.core.windows.net"
```

Link the zone to the VNet:

```
az network private-dns link vnet create \
  --resource-group MyResourceGroup \
  --zone-name "privatelink.blob.core.windows.net" \
```

```
  --name MyDNSLink \
  --virtual-network MyVNet \
  --registration-enabled false
```

Add an A record for the private endpoint:

```
az network private-dns record-set a create \
  --name mystorageacct2025 \
  --zone-name "privatelink.blob.core.windows.net" \
  --resource-group MyResourceGroup
```

DNS Integration

DNS is essential for Private Link to work seamlessly. When a private endpoint is created, Azure automatically generates a FQDN under the `privatelink.*` domain.

To avoid DNS resolution going to the public service, you must:

- Use **Azure** **Private** **DNS** **Zones**

- Override your **on-prem DNS** with conditional forwarding to the private DNS zone

- Avoid hardcoding public IPs or bypassing DNS resolution

This ensures the service name (e.g., `mystorageacct2025.blob.core.windows.net`) resolves to the private IP assigned by Azure.

Private Link Service (PLS)

Private Link Service allows you to expose a custom service in your VNet to consumers in other VNets or tenants.

Use Cases

- SaaS providers offering services via Private Link

- Enterprises segmenting applications across subscriptions

- Zero-trust architectures where front-ends are decoupled from back-end systems

Example: Creating a Private Link Service

1. Deploy your backend service behind an Azure Load Balancer (Standard SKU).

2. Create a Private Link Service pointing to that Load Balancer.

3. The consumer creates a Private Endpoint referencing your PLS.

```
az network private-link-service create \
  --name MyPLS \
  --resource-group MyResourceGroup \
  --vnet-name MyVNet \
  --subnet MySubnet \
  --load-balancer MyLB \
  --frontend-ip-configs MyFrontend \
  --location eastus
```

You can approve connection requests either automatically or manually.

Security Considerations

- **NSGs**: You can associate NSGs with the subnet where the Private Endpoint resides to restrict inbound/outbound traffic.

- **Azure Firewall/NVA**: Use UDRs to inspect or filter traffic to private endpoints.

- **Disable Public Access**: For services like Azure Storage or Key Vault, disable public network access after creating the private endpoint.

```
az storage account update \
  --name mystorageacct2025 \
  --resource-group MyResourceGroup \
  --default-action Deny
```

- **Service Endpoint Policies**: Private Link is preferred over service endpoints for more granular control.

Monitoring and Diagnostics

Monitor Private Endpoint connections using Azure Monitor and Network Watcher.

Log Analytics Example

```
AzureDiagnostics
| where ResourceType == "PRIVATEENDPOINTCONNECTIONS"
| summarize count() by ActivityStatus_s, bin(TimeGenerated, 1h)
```

Connection State Check

```
az network private-endpoint-connection list \
  --resource-group MyResourceGroup \
  --name mystorageacct2025 \
  --type Microsoft.Storage/storageAccounts
```

Traffic Monitoring

Use Network Security Group flow logs and Traffic Analytics to see:

- Who is connecting to the private endpoint

- Source and destination IPs

- Bytes transferred

Hybrid Integration

Private Link works seamlessly in hybrid environments:

- On-prem clients can access Azure services through **VPN or ExpressRoute** using private endpoints

- DNS forwarding must be configured on-prem to resolve the privatelink domain

- Combine with Azure Firewall to monitor and control traffic

This enables architectures such as:

- Secure file backups from on-prem servers to Azure Blob Storage via Private Link

- Key Vault integration with CI/CD pipelines from on-prem build servers

- SQL Server replication from on-prem to Azure SQL using a private endpoint

Best Practices

1. **Use Private Link wherever possible** over service endpoints for stronger security

2. **Integrate with Azure Policy** to enforce Private Link usage across resources

3. **Configure DNS centrally** and avoid split-brain resolution issues

4. **Limit exposure**: Disable public network access on services when Private Link is used

5. **Use Tags** to manage and track Private Endpoints at scale

6. **Audit connections** regularly using Azure Monitor

7. **Avoid using Private Endpoints for high-volume traffic** unless required, to manage cost and performance

8. **Design with identity and access control**: Private Link restricts network access, but RBAC still governs data-level permissions

Summary

Azure Private Link and Private Endpoints offer a secure and efficient way to connect to Azure services and custom endpoints without exposing them to the public internet. They help organizations build zero-trust architectures, comply with regulatory requirements, and reduce attack surfaces by encapsulating service access within private IP spaces.

Whether you're building hybrid, multi-tenant, or fully isolated workloads, Private Link is a foundational component that strengthens your networking model. With proper DNS configuration, security controls, and observability, Private Link enables scalable and secure cloud networking.

In the next section, we'll explore **Azure Bastion** and how it enables secure, browser-based RDP/SSH access to your VMs without exposing them to the internet.

Azure Bastion and Secure Remote Access

Secure remote access to virtual machines is a fundamental requirement for IT administrators, DevOps engineers, and support teams. In traditional environments, RDP and SSH access is often exposed via public IP addresses, increasing the attack surface and risking unauthorized access. Azure Bastion addresses this challenge by providing **secure, seamless RDP and SSH access to virtual machines directly through the Azure portal**, without the need to expose VMs to the public internet.

Azure Bastion is a fully managed Platform-as-a-Service (PaaS) offering that allows you to connect to your VMs using a browser over HTTPS. It provides a hardened access point within your virtual network and integrates with existing Azure security and monitoring services. This section explores the architecture, deployment, use cases, and security implications of Azure Bastion in both cloud-native and hybrid environments.

Key Features

- **No public IP required** for VMs
- **TLS (SSL) encrypted** browser-based RDP and SSH sessions
- **Integrated with Azure Portal**
- **Supports Azure RBAC and NSG**
- **Automatic scaling** and high availability
- **Session auditing** via Azure Monitor and diagnostic logs
- **IP-based access restrictions** with Azure Firewall or NSGs

How Azure Bastion Works

Azure Bastion is deployed in a dedicated subnet within a virtual network called AzureBastionSubnet. Once deployed, it acts as a jump host for VMs within that VNet or peered VNets.

The typical flow is as follows:

1. User signs in to Azure Portal

2. Selects a VM and clicks "Connect" → "Bastion"

3. Bastion initiates a session via port 443 (HTTPS)

4. The VM responds over its internal IP

5. The session is established inside the browser, without downloading any client software

This removes the need for VPNs, public IPs, or agents on VMs.

Creating Azure Bastion

Step 1: Create a Virtual Network and Subnet

```
az network vnet create \
  --resource-group MyResourceGroup \
  --name MyVNet \
  --address-prefix 10.0.0.0/16 \
  --subnet-name AzureBastionSubnet \
  --subnet-prefix 10.0.1.0/26
```

> The subnet **must** be named `AzureBastionSubnet` and have a prefix size of /27 or larger.

Step 2: Create a Public IP for Bastion

```
az network public-ip create \
  --name MyBastionIP \
  --resource-group MyResourceGroup \
  --sku Standard \
  --allocation-method Static
```

Step 3: Deploy Bastion

```
az network bastion create \
  --name MyBastionHost \
  --resource-group MyResourceGroup \
  --vnet-name MyVNet \
  --public-ip-address MyBastionIP \
  --location eastus
```

Once deployed, you can navigate to any VM in the same VNet and initiate a Bastion session through the Azure Portal UI.

Using Bastion in Practice

Connecting via Bastion

1. Go to the VM in Azure Portal

2. Click "Connect"

3. Select "Bastion" tab

4. Enter credentials (username/password or SSH key)

5. Click "Connect"

Your browser opens a session window directly into the VM.

Supported Authentication

- Username/password (RDP, SSH)

- SSH keys

- Custom ports (for Linux)

- Shared keys (in preview with Just-in-Time access)

Advanced Configuration

Access Across Peered VNets

Azure Bastion supports access to VMs in **peered virtual networks** if:

- Bastion is deployed in the **hub VNet**

- VNet peering allows traffic from Bastion

- NSGs and UDRs allow necessary traffic

This supports **hub-and-spoke architectures**, allowing one Bastion deployment to serve an entire environment.

Example: Enable Bastion Across Peered VNets

```
az network vnet peering create \
  --name SpokeToHub \
  --resource-group MyResourceGroup \
  --vnet-name SpokeVNet \
  --remote-vnet HubVNet \
  --allow-vnet-access
```

Ensure NSG rules allow RDP/SSH from the Bastion host's subnet.

Security Considerations

Azure Bastion significantly enhances security posture for remote access:

1. No Public IPs on VMs

- VMs accessed via Bastion do not need public endpoints

- Reduces attack surface (e.g., brute force or port scanning)

2. Just-in-Time (JIT) Access

- Combine Bastion with **Microsoft Defender for Cloud**

- Enable JIT access to control when users can connect

3. RBAC Integration

- Access is controlled via Azure role assignments

- Examples:

  ○ Reader: Can view VM but not connect

  ○ Virtual Machine Administrator Login: Can initiate sessions

4. NSG and Firewall Rules

- Bastion host requires the following:

  ○ Inbound from Azure Cloud (port 443)

  ○ Outbound to VMs (TCP 22/3389)

- Restrict inbound access to Bastion with IP filtering or firewall

Example NSG for Bastion Subnet

```
az network nsg rule create \
  --nsg-name BastionNSG \
  --resource-group MyResourceGroup \
  --name AllowBastion \
```

```
--priority 100 \
--direction Inbound \
--access Allow \
--protocol Tcp \
--source-address-prefix Internet \
--source-port-range '*' \
--destination-port-range 443 \
--destination-address-prefix '*'
```

Monitoring and Auditing

Azure Bastion integrates with Azure Monitor and diagnostic logs for visibility and compliance.

Enable Diagnostics

```
az monitor diagnostic-settings create \
  --resource                              /subscriptions/<sub-
id>/resourceGroups/MyResourceGroup/providers/Microsoft.Network/basti
onHosts/MyBastionHost \
  --workspace MyLogAnalyticsWorkspace \
  --name BastionDiagnostics \
  --logs '[{"category": "BastionAuditLogs", "enabled": true}]'
```

These logs include:

- Connection   attempts

- Session   duration

- Source   IPs

- Login   outcomes

Sample Query

```
AzureDiagnostics
| where ResourceType == "BASTIONHOSTS"
| summarize count() by CallerIpAddress, bin(TimeGenerated, 1h)
```

This helps identify suspicious access patterns or policy violations.

Bastion Premium Features

Azure Bastion offers optional premium capabilities (currently in preview or rolling out):

- **Native Client Support** – Connect from your local RDP/SSH client using Azure CLI

- **Kerberos Authentication** – Integrated with Azure AD for seamless access

- **File Transfer Support** – Upload/download files over Bastion session (RDP)

- **Session Recording** – For audit and compliance tracking

These features make Bastion even more viable for enterprise environments with strict controls and audit needs.

Hybrid and Enterprise Scenarios

Azure Bastion is well-suited to hybrid deployments:

- Combine Bastion with ExpressRoute or VPN to manage hybrid VM fleets

- Access on-prem resources via Azure-hosted jump boxes behind Bastion

- Use with **Azure Lighthouse** for secure, delegated cross-tenant admin access

Example pattern:

1. Central IT deploys Bastion in a hub VNet

2. Developers use Bastion to connect to VMs across spokes and hybrid VNets

3. Audit logs are centralized in Log Analytics

4. No VM in any environment has a public IP

This reduces risk while maintaining agility and administrative control.

Best Practices

1. **Use Bastion instead of exposing VMs to internet**

2. **Deploy Bastion in hub networks** to support multiple spokes

3. **Restrict user access** with least privilege RBAC roles

4. **Audit all sessions** with diagnostics and alerts

5. **Use Just-in-Time access** to limit exposure windows

6. **Enable NSGs and Azure Firewall** to control egress from Bastion subnet

7. **Regularly rotate credentials** and monitor for anomalies

8. **Tag and group Bastion resources** for clarity and management

Summary

Azure Bastion is a secure, scalable, and fully managed solution for remote access to virtual machines. By removing the need for public IP addresses and exposing RDP/SSH ports, it significantly reduces risk while enhancing usability and governance.

Its integration with role-based access control, diagnostics, peering, and premium features makes it an enterprise-grade solution for managing access to Azure VMs. Whether you're managing a single workload or operating a complex hybrid architecture, Azure Bastion provides a modern approach to secure administration.

In the next chapter, we'll explore **network governance, compliance, and cost management**, covering tools like Azure Policy, Blueprints, and best practices for operational excellence.

Chapter 6: Governance, Compliance, and Cost Management

Network Governance with Azure Policy and Blueprints

In any cloud environment—especially those operating at enterprise scale—consistent and secure network configuration is critical. Without governance controls in place, organizations can experience misconfigured networks, compliance violations, or ballooning costs due to resource sprawl. Azure offers a suite of tools to help with governance and standardization: **Azure Policy** and **Azure Blueprints** are two of the most powerful.

This section explores how these tools can be used to implement and enforce governance in Azure networking, ensuring that your environment adheres to security policies, operational standards, and regulatory requirements.

What Is Azure Governance?

Azure governance refers to the mechanisms and services used to control and enforce the operational boundaries of your Azure subscriptions, resources, and networks. Key governance components include:

- **Resource consistency**: Enforcing naming conventions, regions, and SKUs

- **Security controls**: Limiting open ports, public IPs, or NSG misconfigurations

- **Cost management**: Preventing overprovisioned or unnecessary networking services

- **Compliance enforcement**: Ensuring adherence to industry regulations

Azure Policy and **Azure Blueprints** are central to governance by enabling policy-as-code and repeatable deployments with built-in standards.

Azure Policy Overview

Azure Policy enables you to create, assign, and manage policies that enforce rules and effects on your resources. Policies help ensure resources conform to your organization's standards.

Policy Structure

A policy definition has the following key elements:

- **Display** name

- **Description**

- **Policy** rule (logic in JSON)

- **Effect** (e.g., deny, audit, append, deployIfNotExists)

Common Network Governance Policies

Here are some sample policy scenarios for networking:

Goal	Example Policy
Restrict regions	Only allow resources in eastus and westus2
Enforce tag usage	Ensure all VNets have Environment tag
Prohibit public IPs	Deny creation of public IP resources
Limit NSG rules	Deny inbound traffic on port 3389 (RDP)
Monitor non-compliant VPN gateways	Audit VPN Gateways without diagnostics enabled

Example: Deny Public IPs

```
{
  "if": {
    "field": "type",
    "equals": "Microsoft.Network/publicIPAddresses"
  },
  "then": {
    "effect": "deny"
  }
}
```

This policy ensures developers cannot create public IPs, enforcing use of private access methods like Azure Bastion or Private Endpoints.

Assigning and Managing Policies

You can assign policies at the **subscription, resource group**, or **management group** level.

Assigning a policy:

```
az policy assignment create \
  --name deny-public-ip \
  --scope /subscriptions/<sub-id> \
  --policy <policy-definition-id>
```

You can also group multiple policy definitions into **Initiatives** for large-scale compliance frameworks like ISO 27001 or CIS Benchmarks.

Policy Effects

Azure Policy supports several effects:

- **Deny**:   Prevents   the   request

- **Audit**:   Logs   non-compliant   resources

- **Append**:   Adds   missing   properties

- **DeployIfNotExists**:   Creates   required   resources   (e.g.,   NSG)

- **AuditIfNotExists**:   Logs   if   a   dependent   resource   is   not   found

These effects make it possible to enforce not only security but also operational best practices in networking, such as mandatory diagnostics or centralized logging.

Azure Policy for Networking: Best Practices

1. **Start   with   Audit   Mode**
   Begin   with   audit   to   detect   issues   before   enforcing   deny.

2. **Use   DeployIfNotExists   for   Diagnostics**
   Automatically   enable   flow   logs   or   NSG   logging.

3. **Avoid   Overly   Broad   Deny   Policies**
   Target   specific   resource   types   and   scopes   to   avoid   deployment   failures.

4. **Use** **Parameters** **for** **Reusability**
Define allowed regions, tag values, or port ranges as parameters.

Azure Blueprints Overview

Azure Blueprints allow you to define a repeatable set of Azure resources and policies that implement and adhere to an organization's standards, patterns, and requirements.

Blueprints combine:

- Role-based access control (RBAC)

- Resource templates (ARM)

- Policy assignments

- Resource groups

They are ideal for provisioning environments like **development**, **testing**, or **production** with consistent security and compliance.

Blueprint Anatomy

A blueprint consists of:

- **Artifacts**: Policies, role assignments, resource groups, templates

- **Blueprint definition**: Describes the blueprint structure

- **Blueprint assignment**: Applies the blueprint to a subscription

Example Artifacts:

Type	Purpose
Policy Assignment	Ensure no public IPs are created
Role Assignment	Assign Network Contributor to engineers
ARM Template	Deploy VNet, subnets, NSGs

Resource Group	Organize all network components

Creating and Assigning a Blueprint

1. **Create the blueprint definition**
   In the Azure Portal or via Azure CLI (currently requires REST API/PowerShell for full functionality)

2. **Add artifacts**
   For example:

   - Policy: Deny public IPs

   - Resource Group: Networking-RG

   - ARM Template: Deploy standard NSG

3. **Publish and assign**
   Specify parameters and assign it to a subscription.

```
az blueprint assignment create \
  --name dev-network-blueprint \
  --blueprint-name dev-network \
  --subscription <sub-id> \
  --location eastus
```

Example: Blueprint for a Secured Network Foundation

Artifacts:

- **Policy**: Deny public IPs
- **Policy**: Enforce NSG on all subnets
- **Role**: Reader for security team
- **Template**: Create hub VNet and shared firewall
- **Resource Group**: Core-Networking

Benefits:

- Consistent, secure network foundation for all new environments

- Reduced manual provisioning

- Built-in compliance

Integrating Governance with DevOps

To make governance scalable, integrate Azure Policy and Blueprints with your CI/CD pipelines:

- Use **Azure DevOps** or **GitHub Actions** to deploy policies and blueprint assignments as code

- Store policy definitions in source control

- Automate policy compliance checks during infrastructure deployment

This approach enables a **policy-as-code** model, bringing governance into the development lifecycle.

Monitoring Compliance

Azure Policy integrates with **Azure Security Center** and **Azure Monitor** to report on compliance state.

Check policy compliance:

```
az policy state summarize \
  --management-group <group-id> \
  --query "summary.results"
```

You can create alerts when resources become non-compliant and view detailed remediation guidance in the Azure Portal.

Remediation and Auto-Fix

Azure Policy supports **automatic remediation** for certain policy types, especially DeployIfNotExists. You can create remediation tasks to apply missing configurations.

Example: Ensure all VNets have NSG

- Policy: `DeployIfNotExists` for NSG on each subnet

- Remediation task: Attach NSG to non-compliant subnets

```
az policy remediation create \
  --name remediate-missing-nsgs \
  --scope /subscriptions/<sub-id> \
  --policy-assignment <assignment-id>
```

Summary

Azure Policy and Azure Blueprints provide essential tools for enforcing network governance across cloud environments. With these tools, organizations can prevent misconfigurations, maintain compliance, and streamline provisioning of secure and standardized infrastructure.

- Use **Azure Policy** to control individual configurations like public IPs or NSGs

- Use **Azure Blueprints** to deploy entire network environments with built-in policies and structure

- Integrate governance into DevOps pipelines to ensure consistency from development through production

- Monitor compliance continuously and remediate issues automatically where possible

In the next section, we'll explore how to meet regulatory and industry-specific **compliance requirements**, including those for healthcare, finance, and government workloads running in Azure.

Compliance Considerations for Regulated Industries

In regulated industries such as finance, healthcare, energy, and government, compliance is not optional—it is a foundational requirement. Organizations must meet stringent legal and regulatory standards for data handling, network security, access control, and auditing. Azure provides a comprehensive set of tools, certifications, and architectural options to help meet these requirements while building secure, scalable, and compliant network infrastructures.

This section explores how regulated industries can leverage Azure's native capabilities to architect, monitor, and maintain compliant network environments, ensuring adherence to frameworks such as HIPAA, GDPR, PCI-DSS, ISO 27001, FedRAMP, and others.

Regulatory Frameworks and Azure Alignment

Azure maintains a deep portfolio of certifications that map to common compliance frameworks around the globe. Some key ones include:

Regulation/Framework	Description
HIPAA	U.S. health information privacy and security law
GDPR	European Union regulation on data protection and privacy
PCI-DSS	Payment Card Industry standard for credit card processing
ISO/IEC 27001	International standard for information security management
FedRAMP	U.S. government security assessment framework for cloud providers
CJIS	U.S. law enforcement standard for criminal justice information systems
NIST 800-53	U.S. cybersecurity framework used by federal agencies

Microsoft Azure provides **compliance blueprints**, **compliance documentation**, and **prebuilt policy initiatives** that help map technical implementation to specific controls.

Core Networking Compliance Challenges

In regulated environments, network-related compliance mandates typically include:

- **Data residency**: Ensuring data is stored and processed in approved geographies
- **Network segmentation**: Isolating sensitive workloads from general purpose or public networks
- **Zero-trust access**: Strict authentication and authorization
- **Traffic inspection**: Monitoring and logging of inbound and outbound traffic

- **Auditability**: Complete visibility into changes, connections, and access logs

- **Encryption   in   transit   and   at   rest**

Azure networking provides native services to address all of these concerns through architectural patterns, policy enforcement, and integration with logging and monitoring tools.

Data Residency and Sovereignty

Azure has over 60 regions globally and allows customers to control **data residency** by selecting specific regions when deploying resources. For sensitive workloads:

- Deploy in **region-specific** or **sovereign clouds** (e.g., Azure Government, Azure Germany,   Azure   China)

- Use **availability zones** within compliant regions for redundancy without leaving jurisdiction

- Implement **Private Link** to ensure traffic remains on the Microsoft backbone and does not   traverse   the   public   internet

  For GDPR and similar mandates, avoid cross-border data flows by controlling where data is accessed and processed.

Network Segmentation and Isolation

Regulated workloads must be isolated to prevent lateral movement and data leakage. Azure supports this through:

1. Hub-and-Spoke Topology

- Centralized   management   and   security   in   the   hub   (firewalls,   logging)

- Workload   isolation   in   spokes   (per   environment   or   tenant)

- Enforce   NSGs   and   UDRs   to   limit   connectivity

2. Virtual Network Service Endpoints and Private Link

- Access   PaaS   services   (e.g.,   Azure   SQL,   Storage)   privately

- Prevent services from being accessible over public IPs

3. Application Gateway with WAF

- Protect web applications with OWASP rules
- Provide routing and application-layer inspection

4. ExpressRoute and VPN Gateways

- Secure hybrid connectivity using encrypted or private links
- Supports scenarios like disaster recovery and cross-prem compliance zones

---

Access Control and Zero Trust

Zero Trust is a principle where **no entity is trusted by default**—identity, device, and context must be validated continuously. In Azure:

- **Azure AD** controls user identity and access management
- **Role-Based Access Control (RBAC)** restricts who can manage and connect to resources
- **Conditional Access Policies** restrict access by user, location, device health
- **Privileged Identity Management (PIM)** provides just-in-time access with approval workflows
- **Azure Bastion** enables secure RDP/SSH without exposing VMs to the internet

For regulated workloads, combine these tools to:

- Enforce least privilege access
- Prevent persistent admin roles
- Require MFA and session approval

Traffic Inspection and Logging

Compliance frameworks often require **visibility into all traffic,** including access attempts, protocol usage, and potential anomalies.

Tools for Traffic Logging:

Tool	Purpose
NSG Flow Logs	Capture 5-tuple network flow metadata
Azure Firewall Logs	Log all allowed/denied connections, threats
Packet Capture	Capture raw packet data for detailed inspection
Application Gateway Logs	HTTP requests and WAF hits
Connection Monitor	Visualize traffic flows and path validation

Enabling NSG Flow Logs:

```
az network watcher flow-log configure \
  --resource-group MyResourceGroup \
  --nsg-name MyNSG \
  --enabled true \
  --storage-account mystorageacct \
  --retention 30
```

These logs can be ingested into **Log Analytics** and queried with **Kusto** for compliance audits and threat hunting.

Encryption in Transit and at Rest

Many compliance standards mandate encryption for sensitive data:

- **In Transit**: Use HTTPS, IPsec VPN, or ExpressRoute encryption

- **At Rest**: Azure encrypts all data at rest by default (Storage, SQL, etc.)

For added control:

- Use **Customer-Managed Keys (CMK)** with Azure Key Vault

- Enable **TLS 1.2+ only** on all public-facing endpoints
- For workloads handling sensitive information, enable **end-to-end encryption** (TLS on frontend and backend)

Regulatory Blueprints and Policy Initiatives

Azure provides **pre-built initiatives** that bundle together dozens of policies mapped to specific compliance controls.

Examples:

Blueprint/Initiative Name	Description
NIST SP 800-53 R4	U.S. Federal baseline
HIPAA/HITRUST	Healthcare compliance for U.S.
PCI-DSS v3.2.1	Payment card compliance
UK OFFICIAL	Government cloud standard for the UK
ISO 27001:2013	International security baseline

You can assign these initiatives at the subscription or management group level.

Assigning an Initiative:

```
az policy assignment create \
  --name pci-dss-compliance \
  --scope /subscriptions/<sub-id> \
  --policy-set-definition <policySetId> \
  --location eastus
```

Initiatives also track **compliance score**, showing which resources are compliant and why others are not.

Auditing and Continuous Compliance

Azure provides native tools for ongoing auditing:

- **Azure Policy Compliance Reports**
- **Microsoft Defender for Cloud** regulatory scorecards
- **Activity Logs** to track changes
- **Azure Monitor Alerts** for violations or unusual traffic

Sample Kusto Query for NSG Violations:

```
AzureDiagnostics
| where Resource == "NETWORKSECURITYGROUPS"
| where msg_s contains "Deny"
| summarize count() by SourceIP, DestinationPort, bin(TimeGenerated,
1h)
```

You can also use **Azure Sentinel** for extended SIEM functionality across hybrid environments.

Best Practices for Regulated Industries

1. **Use Private Link and disable public access**
2. **Implement RBAC and PIM across all roles**
3. **Log everything**—flow logs, DNS queries, firewall rules
4. **Use Blueprints for repeatable compliance**
5. **Regularly audit access logs and NSG flows**
6. **Encrypt everywhere**—at rest, in transit, and in use (Confidential Computing)
7. **Use sovereign cloud if applicable** (e.g., Azure Government)
8. **Apply policy-as-code** principles via DevOps pipelines
9. **Monitor regulatory compliance score** in Defender for Cloud
10. **Enable diagnostics on all networking components**

Summary

Compliance is a continuous journey, not a one-time goal. In regulated industries, the network is often the first layer of defense—and the first subject of scrutiny. Azure provides the tooling, controls, and certifications needed to meet even the most demanding requirements across finance, healthcare, government, and beyond.

By leveraging Private Link, RBAC, NSG policies, diagnostics, encryption, and the Azure Policy framework, organizations can build cloud architectures that not only meet compliance today but are resilient and auditable for the future.

In the next section, we'll explore cost optimization strategies for networking components—ensuring that secure and compliant doesn't mean unnecessarily expensive.

Cost Optimization for Network Resources

As workloads scale in Azure, networking costs can become a significant component of overall cloud spend. These expenses are often hidden across different services—bandwidth egress, VPN gateways, public IPs, load balancers, firewalls, private endpoints, and third-party network appliances. Without deliberate cost management, organizations may overspend on underutilized or misconfigured networking resources.

This section focuses on understanding the cost model of Azure networking, identifying common cost drivers, and applying practical strategies and tools to optimize for performance **and** budget. The goal is not to reduce security or availability but to achieve them in the most cost-effective way possible.

Understanding Azure Networking Cost Components

Networking costs in Azure can be categorized into several key areas:

Cost Area	Description
Egress Bandwidth	Data leaving Azure to the internet, other regions, or on-prem
Load Balancers	Costs vary by SKU and rules used (Standard vs Basic)
Public IP Addresses	Static IPs and Standard SKUs incur charges
VPN and ExpressRoute Gateways	Per-hour and per-GB charges apply
Private Endpoints and Link	Per-connection and data processing charges

Network Security Appliances   VM-based or marketplace appliances with licensing

DNS Queries   Managed DNS zones incur usage-based fees

Ingress (incoming traffic to Azure) is generally free.

Common Sources of Waste and Overspend

1. **Overprovisioned**   **Gateways**
   Many organizations deploy higher-tier VPN or ExpressRoute gateways than needed.

2. **Idle**   **or**   **Static**   **Public**   **IPs**
   Public IPs assigned to stopped VMs or unused services still incur charges.

3. **Unnecessary**   **Cross-Region**   **Traffic**
   Applications architected poorly may send traffic between regions when it could be localized.

4. **Improper**   **Load**   **Balancer**   **SKUs**
   Standard SKU may be used where Basic is sufficient—or vice versa, incurring unintended fees or under-delivering.

5. **Underutilized**   **or**   **forgotten**   **Private**   **Endpoints**
   Each Private Endpoint incurs charges—even if unused.

6. **Third-party**   **appliances**
   Marketplace solutions such as firewalls can be cost-prohibitive if not properly sized or rightsized.

7. **Custom**   **DNS**   **and**   **Traffic**   **Manager**   **usage**
   Using features like Traffic Manager across regions without understanding traffic flow can result in unnecessary global egress.

Key Strategies for Networking Cost Optimization

1. Review and Right-Size Network Gateways

Each tier of VPN or ExpressRoute gateway has a different per-hour and throughput-based cost.

Gateway Tier	Monthly Cost (est.)	Max Throughput
VpnGw1	~$100	650 Mbps
VpnGw2	~$200	1 Gbps
VpnGw5	~$950	10 Gbps

Action: Use monitoring tools to evaluate actual bandwidth usage and downgrade where appropriate.

```
az monitor metrics list \
  --resource                         /subscriptions/<sub-
id>/resourceGroups/MyRG/providers/Microsoft.Network/virtualNetworkGa
teways/MyVPN \
  --metric-name TunnelBandwidthIn
```

2. Consolidate Load Balancers and Reduce Rules

Each load balancing rule in **Standard Load Balancer** incurs a small cost. Over time, this adds up—especially in microservice environments.

- Evaluate merging backend pools and routing rules

- Use **Basic Load Balancer** for development or non-critical workloads

- Consider Application Gateway for HTTP/HTTPS traffic with WAF to reduce extra components

3. Audit and Reclaim Unused Public IPs

Run regular audits to identify IPs attached to deallocated or orphaned resources.

```
az network public-ip list --query "[?ipAddress && !ipConfiguration]"
-o table
```

Releasing unused IPs helps reduce cost and avoids hitting IP quota limits.

4. Use Azure Hybrid Benefit for Network Appliances

If deploying third-party firewalls (e.g., Palo Alto, Fortinet), leverage **Azure Hybrid Benefit** or use BYOL (Bring Your Own License) models where applicable. Prepaid licenses can significantly reduce monthly costs.

Additionally:

- Use **Autoscaling features** on appliances
- Run them only during business hours if not critical 24/7
- Prefer **Azure Firewall** for consistent pricing and native integration

---

5. Optimize Egress Costs

Traffic flowing **out** of Azure can get expensive quickly:

Destination	Approx. Cost (per GB)
Internet	$0.087
Another Azure region	$0.02 - $0.05
On-prem via VPN	$0.035
On-prem via ER	$0.025

Strategies to reduce egress:

- Keep resources in the **same region**
- Use **Content Delivery Network (CDN)** for static assets
- Implement **caching** in front-end apps
- Use **ExpressRoute Local** to avoid unnecessary routing
- Compress payloads and optimize chatty protocols

---

6. Monitor Private Endpoint Usage

Private Endpoints are billed for:

- Hours   provisioned

- Data   processed   through   the   connection

For low-traffic services, consider **Service Endpoints** instead—especially if compliance requirements don't prohibit them.

Use policy to detect and control proliferation:

```
{
  "if": {
    "field": "type",
    "equals": "Microsoft.Network/privateEndpoints"
  },
  "then": {
    "effect": "audit"
  }
}
```

7. Set Up Alerts and Budgets

Use Azure Cost Management and Azure Monitor to create budgets and alert thresholds.

Creating a budget:

```
az consumption budget create \
  --name network-budget \
  --amount 1000 \
  --category cost \
  --time-grain Monthly \
  --resource-group MyResourceGroup \
  --time-period start=2025-01-01T00:00:00Z end=2025-12-31T23:59:59Z \
  --notifications '[{"enabled": true, "operator": "GreaterThan",
"threshold": 90, "contactEmails": ["ops@company.com"]}]'
```

This helps prevent budget surprises and promotes proactive cost control.

8. Apply Cost-Conscious Governance

Leverage Azure Policy to enforce best practices such as:

- Disallow public IPs in non-production environments
- Deny deployment of higher-cost SKU Load Balancers without approval
- Require tagging (e.g., Environment, CostCenter, Project) for cost attribution

Example: Deny Standard Public IPs in dev environments

```json
{
  "if": {
    "allOf": [
      {
        "field": "type",
        "equals": "Microsoft.Network/publicIPAddresses"
      },
      {
        "field": "Microsoft.Resources.tags.Environment",
        "equals": "Development"
      },
      {
        "field": "Microsoft.Network/publicIPAddresses.sku.name",
        "equals": "Standard"
      }
    ]
  },
  "then": {
    "effect": "deny"
  }
}
```

Monitoring Tools for Cost Optimization

Azure provides several tools for analyzing and managing network cost:

Tool	Purpose
Azure Cost Analysis	View cost by service, region, resource

Network Watcher	Analyze data transfer patterns
Azure Advisor	Recommendations for underutilized resources
Azure Pricing Calculator	Estimate cost impact of new deployments
Log Analytics	Custom queries on usage metrics

Use these tools regularly to spot trends and forecast impact of planned changes.

Dev/Test and Non-Prod Network Savings

- Use **Auto-shutdown** on bastion hosts and appliances
- Use **Basic SKU** where HA is not required
- Use **free tier** DNS and peering features for low-volume environments
- **Disable diagnostics temporarily** if verbose logging isn't necessary

Always separate prod and non-prod environments by resource group or subscription for clear cost visibility and governance.

Summary

Cost optimization in Azure networking is not about cutting corners—it's about strategic design, vigilant monitoring, and smart automation. By understanding where costs originate and enforcing a culture of fiscal responsibility, teams can build robust, performant networks without overspending.

To recap:

- Right-size gateways and load balancers
- Reduce egress by localizing architecture
- Eliminate unused or misconfigured public IPs
- Use automation and policy to enforce cost-aware deployments

- Monitor continuously and act early

In the next section, we'll explore how to automate network configuration and governance using Azure CLI, PowerShell, and the Bicep infrastructure-as-code language for repeatable and auditable deployments.

Automation with Azure CLI, PowerShell, and Bicep

As cloud environments scale, manual configuration and maintenance become unsustainable and error-prone. Automation is essential for maintaining consistent, secure, and governed network infrastructure across development, staging, and production environments. In Azure, three primary tools support infrastructure automation: **Azure CLI**, **Azure PowerShell**, and **Bicep**.

This section explores how these tools can be used to automate Azure networking tasks—such as provisioning virtual networks, configuring security, deploying gateways, and applying policies—with reusable, modular, and version-controlled code. You'll learn how to structure your automation strategy for scalability, compliance, and long-term maintainability.

Why Automate Azure Networking?

Manual network configuration has several pitfalls:

- **Human error** (e.g., misconfigured NSG rules)
- **Inconsistency** across environments
- **Time-consuming** deployments
- **Hard** to audit or reproduce

Automation helps solve these by enabling:

- **Declarative** provisioning
- **Version-controlled** infrastructure
- **Rapid** environment replication
- **Integrated** CI/CD pipelines

Azure CLI Overview

Azure CLI is a cross-platform command-line tool that provides access to Azure resources. It is ideal for scripting tasks, creating resources, and querying configurations.

Key benefits:

- Available   on   all   OS   platforms

- Lightweight   and   fast

- Easily   integrates   with   scripts   and   DevOps   pipelines

Example: Deploying a VNet with CLI

```
az network vnet create \
  --name MyVNet \
  --resource-group MyResourceGroup \
  --location eastus \
  --address-prefix 10.1.0.0/16 \
  --subnet-name MySubnet \
  --subnet-prefix 10.1.1.0/24
```

Example: Configuring NSG with CLI

```
az network nsg create \
  --resource-group MyResourceGroup \
  --name MyNSG

az network nsg rule create \
  --resource-group MyResourceGroup \
  --nsg-name MyNSG \
  --name AllowSSH \
  --protocol Tcp \
  --direction Inbound \
  --priority 100 \
  --source-address-prefixes '*' \
  --destination-port-ranges 22 \
  --access Allow
```

CLI is especially effective when used in **Bash scripts** for repeatable network deployments or operational automation.

Azure PowerShell Overview

Azure PowerShell is a task automation framework tailored for IT admins and Windows environments. It provides full parity with Azure CLI but uses cmdlets instead of shell-style commands.

Benefits:

- Ideal for Windows admins and hybrid environments
- Integrates with existing PowerShell scripts
- Useful for automation within **Azure Automation** or **Function Apps**

Example: Creating a VNet and Subnet in PowerShell

```
$vnet = New-AzVirtualNetwork `
  -Name "MyVNet" `
  -ResourceGroupName "MyResourceGroup" `
  -Location "EastUS" `
  -AddressPrefix "10.1.0.0/16"

Add-AzVirtualNetworkSubnetConfig `
  -Name "MySubnet" `
  -AddressPrefix "10.1.1.0/24" `
  -VirtualNetwork $vnet

$vnet | Set-AzVirtualNetwork
```

Example: Assigning an NSG to a Subnet

```
$nsg = New-AzNetworkSecurityGroup `
  -ResourceGroupName "MyResourceGroup" `
  -Location "EastUS" `
  -Name "MyNSG"

$subnetConfig = Get-AzVirtualNetworkSubnetConfig -VirtualNetwork $vnet -Name "MySubnet"
$subnetConfig.NetworkSecurityGroup = $nsg
Set-AzVirtualNetwork -VirtualNetwork $vnet
```

PowerShell is well-suited to enterprise IT teams managing complex, hybrid network setups.

Bicep: The Infrastructure-as-Code Language for Azure

Bicep is a domain-specific language (DSL) that simplifies the authoring of ARM templates. It is **declarative**, **modular**, **reusable**, and **cleaner** than raw JSON.

Bicep enables:

- Modular network definitions (VNets, subnets, NSGs, etc.)

- Parameterized deployments

- Reusability across environments

- Integration with CI/CD and DevOps platforms

Example: Bicep Template for a VNet with Subnet and NSG

```
param location string = 'eastus'
param vnetName string = 'myVnet'
param subnetName string = 'mySubnet'
param addressPrefix string = '10.1.0.0/16'
param subnetPrefix string = '10.1.1.0/24'

resource vnet 'Microsoft.Network/virtualNetworks@2021-05-01' = {
  name: vnetName
  location: location
  properties: {
    addressSpace: {
      addressPrefixes: [addressPrefix]
    }
    subnets: [
      {
        name: subnetName
        properties: {
          addressPrefix: subnetPrefix
          networkSecurityGroup: {
            id: nsg.id
          }
        }
      }
    ]
  }
}
```

```
resource nsg 'Microsoft.Network/networkSecurityGroups@2021-05-01' = {
  name: 'myNSG'
  location: location
  properties: {
    securityRules: [
      {
        name: 'AllowSSH'
        properties: {
          priority: 100
          direction: 'Inbound'
          access: 'Allow'
          protocol: 'Tcp'
          sourceAddressPrefix: '*'
          sourcePortRange: '*'
          destinationAddressPrefix: '*'
          destinationPortRange: '22'
        }
      }
    ]
  }
}
```

Deploy the Bicep File

```
az deployment group create \
  --resource-group MyResourceGroup \
  --template-file ./networking.bicep
```

Automating Network Security

Use Bicep or scripting tools to:

- **Enforce NSGs on every subnet**
- **Ensure flow logs are enabled**
- **Apply Azure Firewall route tables**
- **Deploy Application Gateway with WAF rules**
- **Create policies and assign them automatically**

You can combine Bicep with **Azure Policy** to ensure that automated resources are compliant from day one.

CI/CD Integration

Azure CLI, PowerShell, and Bicep are easily integrated into:

- **GitHub** **Actions**
- **Azure** **DevOps** **Pipelines**
- **Terraform** **workflows** **(hybrid)**
- **Jenkins** or **TeamCity** **scripts**

Example GitHub Actions workflow for Bicep deployment:

```
jobs:
  deploy:
    runs-on: ubuntu-latest
    steps:
    - uses: actions/checkout@v2
    - name: Azure Login
      uses: azure/login@v1
      with:
        creds: ${{ secrets.AZURE_CREDENTIALS }}
    - name: Deploy Bicep
      run: |
        az deployment group create \
          --resource-group MyResourceGroup \
          --template-file ./main.bicep
```

Automated deployments ensure consistency and speed across environments.

Version Control and Collaboration

Store your automation scripts and Bicep files in **Git repositories**:

- Promote collaboration through pull requests and reviews

- Enforce quality with linters (e.g., `bicep` `lint`)
- Roll back failed deployments quickly
- Create environment-specific branches

Always use parameter files to separate logic from configuration, especially for multi-environment deployments.

Testing and Validation

Use the following tools to validate templates before deploying:

- `az` `deployment` `what-if` – Preview changes
- `bicep` `build` – Compile to ARM JSON
- `bicep` `decompile` – Convert ARM to Bicep
- `Test-AzResourceGroupDeployment` – Validate PowerShell scripts

Regular testing in CI pipelines helps catch configuration drift and syntax issues early.

Best Practices

1. **Use Bicep for declarative infrastructure-as-code**
2. **Modularize** your templates (VNet, NSG, Route Table, etc.)
3. **Integrate automation into your CI/CD pipeline**
4. **Parameterize everything**—avoid hardcoded values
5. **Include tagging automation** for resource tracking
6. **Enable diagnostics and logging by default**
7. **Use automation to enforce governance and compliance**
8. **Use** `az monitor` **and** `az policy` **in scripts** to validate environment post-deployment

Summary

Automation is the cornerstone of cloud-scale network management. Azure CLI, PowerShell, and Bicep provide a powerful trio for provisioning, managing, and governing networking resources in Azure. By adopting infrastructure-as-code practices, teams can build resilient, secure, and reproducible environments that align with business requirements and compliance standards.

Through automation, you achieve not only operational efficiency but also stronger governance, improved auditability, and faster time-to-delivery for infrastructure changes.

In the next chapter, we'll shift focus to **architecting resilient and scalable networks**, including redundancy models, multi-region designs, and performance optimization strategies.

Chapter 7: Architecting for Resilience and Scalability

Designing Redundant and Highly Available Networks

Designing for resilience and high availability is a critical aspect of network architecture in Azure. As applications move to the cloud, users expect continuous uptime, rapid failover, and seamless service delivery—regardless of regional outages, maintenance events, or spikes in demand. To meet these expectations, network architectures must be built to withstand component failures, geographic disruptions, and resource bottlenecks.

This section explores the principles, patterns, and Azure-native tools required to build **redundant**, **fault-tolerant**, and **highly available** network infrastructures. You'll learn how to implement multi-tier designs, leverage availability zones and regions, implement active-active topologies, and use load balancers and route control to support high-uptime environments.

Principles of Highly Available Network Design

1. **Eliminate   Single   Points   of   Failure   (SPOF)**
   Redundancy must be applied at every critical layer—compute, network, and application.

2. **Fault   Isolation**
   Use segmentation (e.g., VNets, subnets, NSGs) to prevent failure propagation.

3. **Fail   Fast   and   Recover   Fast**
   Use health probes, monitoring, and automation to detect and resolve issues quickly.

4. **Scale   Independently**
   Each tier (e.g., frontend, app, data) should scale on its own to avoid cascading failures.

5. **Predictable   Performance**
   Design for low-latency and high-throughput with minimal jitter and congestion.

Availability Zones and Regional Redundancy

Azure provides **Availability Zones (AZs)** within supported regions. Each zone is an isolated data center with independent power, cooling, and networking.

Redundant Network Components with AZs:

- **Virtual Network Gateways**: Zone-redundant gateways support active-active configurations.

- **Azure Load Balancer**: Standard SKU supports zone-aware frontends.

- **Azure Firewall**: Deploy in active-active HA with zone support.

- **Application Gateway**: v2 SKU supports zone redundancy.

- **Public IPs**: Standard IPs can be zone-redundant.

Example: Creating a Zone-Redundant Load Balancer

```
az network public-ip create \
  --resource-group MyResourceGroup \
  --name MyZonalIP \
  --sku Standard \
  --allocation-method static \
  --zone 1 2 3
```

Use the same zones in the Load Balancer or App Gateway deployment to achieve full redundancy.

Redundant VPN and ExpressRoute Gateways

Active-Active VPN Gateway

Use multiple VPN tunnels in an **active-active configuration** for high availability.

```
az network vnet-gateway create \
  --name MyVPNGateway \
  --resource-group MyResourceGroup \
  --vnet MyVNet \
  --public-ip-addresses MyPublicIP1 MyPublicIP2 \
  --gateway-type Vpn \
  --vpn-type RouteBased \
  --sku VpnGw2 \
  --active-active true
```

- Deploy BGP to automatically failover connections.

- Use multiple on-premises VPN devices for redundancy.

ExpressRoute Resiliency Models

Model	Description
Basic	Single circuit, single peering
High Availability	Dual connections from same provider
Geo-Redundant	Two circuits in different metros for disaster recovery

Use **ExpressRoute FastPath** and **Private Peering** for lowest-latency and highest-throughput needs.

Application-Level Redundancy

Implementing redundancy above the network layer ensures your apps remain available even if underlying components fail.

Use Azure Load Balancer (L4)

- Distributes TCP/UDP traffic across multiple VMs
- Use with Availability Sets or VM Scale Sets
- Health probes automatically reroute traffic from unhealthy instances

Use Azure Application Gateway (L7)

- Offers intelligent routing, path-based routing, SSL termination, WAF
- Ideal for web apps, microservices, and APIs

Use Azure Traffic Manager (DNS)

- Provides global traffic routing
- Supports Priority, Weighted, Performance, and Geographic routing

Example: Priority-based failover

```
az network traffic-manager profile create \
  --name MyAppFailover \
  --resource-group MyResourceGroup \
  --routing-method Priority \
  --unique-dns-name myappglobaldns \
  --monitor-path "/" \
  --monitor-protocol HTTP \
  --monitor-port 80
```

Combine **Traffic Manager + Load Balancer** to implement regional and local redundancy.

Hub-and-Spoke Architecture for Network Redundancy

Hub-and-Spoke enables scalable and centralized control over networking services.

- **Hub VNet**: Shared resources like firewalls, VPN/ER gateways, DNS

- **Spoke VNets**: Isolated workloads or applications

- **Peering**: Use VNet peering with useRemoteGateways for shared access

Advantages:

- Easier to secure and monitor traffic centrally

- Isolates failures within individual spokes

- Supports global scalability

Add NVA (e.g., Palo Alto, Cisco) or Azure Firewall in the hub for secure, redundant egress and inspection.

Redundant Subnet and NSG Design

Segment subnets by tier or function:

- Web Tier (public)

- App Tier (private)

- Data   Tier   (isolated)

Apply NSGs per subnet for security boundaries. To ensure availability:

- Deploy   multiple   instances   of   each   tier   across   zones
- Associate   redundant   route   tables   or   NSGs   across   subnets
- Use   **UDRs**   to   route   through   NVAs   or   Firewall

Example: UDR to route traffic through Firewall

```
az network route-table route create \
  --resource-group MyResourceGroup \
  --route-table-name MyRouteTable \
  --name RouteToFirewall \
  --address-prefix 0.0.0.0/0 \
  --next-hop-type VirtualAppliance \
  --next-hop-ip-address 10.0.0.4
```

High Availability with Azure Firewall

Azure Firewall supports:

- **Active-Active**   **mode**
- **Availability**   **Zones**
- **Autoscaling**
- **Forced**   **tunneling**
- **HA**   **with**   **multiple**   **UDR**   **paths**

Example deployment with zone redundancy:

```
az network firewall create \
  --name MyFirewall \
  --resource-group MyResourceGroup \
  --location eastus \
  --sku AZFW_VNet \
  --zones 1 2 3
```

Use health probes, NSG logs, and Firewall logs to monitor and route based on service health.

Monitoring and Health Probing

Use **Azure Monitor**, **Log Analytics**, and **Network Watcher** to track:

- Load balancer probe failures
- VPN tunnel status
- ExpressRoute BGP sessions
- NSG and Firewall logs
- Application Gateway backend pool health

Create alerts to trigger remediation scripts or autoscaling actions.

Sample Kusto query to detect repeated VPN disconnects:

```
AzureDiagnostics
| where ResourceType == "VPNCONNECTIONS"
| where Category == "TunnelDiagnosticLog"
| summarize Disconnects = count() by Computer, bin(TimeGenerated, 1h)
| where Disconnects > 5
```

Geographic Redundancy and Disaster Recovery

Plan for **regional outages** by deploying across two or more Azure regions.

- Use **paired regions** for compliance and replication
- Deploy identical environments in each region
- Use **Azure Front Door** or **Traffic Manager** for global failover
- Replicate stateful data using **Geo-Replication** (SQL, Storage, Cosmos DB)

Blueprint pattern:

- East US primary, West US secondary
- Primary DNS via Traffic Manager with automatic failover
- Load Balancer and Gateway in each region
- Use BGP failover for hybrid routing back to on-prem

Testing Resilience

You cannot assume availability without testing. Introduce **failure injection** and **chaos engineering**:

- Shut down a gateway instance
- Kill traffic on one subnet
- Simulate regional failure (e.g., disable routing)
- Use Azure Chaos Studio to automate testing

Practice incident response for failover, rollback, and reroute procedures.

Best Practices

1. **Use AZs for in-region HA**
2. **Use paired regions for DR**
3. **Design for failover with Traffic Manager or Front Door**
4. **Avoid single instances of load balancers, firewalls, VMs**
5. **Monitor health continuously and probe every service**
6. **Separate critical paths from non-critical (telemetry, backup)**
7. **Test failure scenarios regularly**
8. **Tag and document all HA components**

9. **Automate deployment of redundant resources with Bicep or Terraform**

10. **Ensure budget for redundancy—cost of downtime is higher**

Summary

Redundancy and high availability are not add-ons—they are core design principles in cloud-native architecture. Azure offers a rich toolkit for building robust networks that remain available even during failures, upgrades, or high traffic events.

From Availability Zones and Load Balancers to Traffic Manager and ExpressRoute resiliency, you can combine these tools to meet the uptime requirements of any workload, in any industry.

In the next section, we'll explore how to extend these concepts into **multi-region and global network designs**, enabling truly scalable, globally available applications and services.

Multi-region and Global Network Design

Designing a multi-region and globally distributed network in Azure is essential for achieving geographic redundancy, regulatory compliance, performance optimization, and seamless customer experiences. As businesses expand their digital footprint, applications must be architected to remain resilient, secure, and performant across multiple Azure regions and, often, around the world.

This section details the strategies, architectures, and Azure-native services that support global network design. It covers region pairing, inter-region connectivity, global load balancing, DNS-based routing, data replication considerations, and design patterns for applications that must operate across continents without compromise.

Goals of Multi-region Network Design

A well-architected global network should meet the following objectives:

1. **High   Availability**
   The application remains available during regional outages or service failures.

2. **Disaster   Recovery   (DR)**
   A designated region can take over in case of catastrophic failure.

3. **Low   Latency**
   Users are routed to the closest region for the best performance.

4. **Regulatory**   **Compliance**
Data is processed and stored in approved regions based on residency laws.

5. **Scalability**
The architecture must support rapid expansion to new geographies.

6. **Operational**   **Efficiency**
Resources and configurations are centralized where beneficial and decentralized where required.

Azure Region Architecture Concepts

Azure consists of **geographies**, **regions**, and **availability zones**:

- **Geography**: A sovereign area, such as the U.S. or EU.

- **Region**: A specific Azure datacenter cluster (e.g., East US, West Europe).

- **Paired Regions**: Two regions within a geography paired for DR and update sequencing.

Benefits of Paired Regions

- Data residency guarantees within same geography

- Asynchronous replication for services like Storage and SQL

- Coordinated updates to minimize downtime

- Priority recovery in case of a region-wide outage

Example Paired Regions:

- East US ↔ West US

- North Europe ↔ West Europe

- Japan East ↔ Japan West

Global Virtual Network Design

You can interconnect virtual networks across regions using:

- **Global** **VNet** **Peering**
- **Virtual** **WAN**
- **ExpressRoute** **Global** **Reach**

1. Global VNet Peering

Allows you to connect VNets across regions using Azure's private backbone with minimal latency.

```
az network vnet peering create \
  --name EastToWest \
  --resource-group RG-East \
  --vnet-name VNet-East \
  --remote-vnet VNet-West \
  --allow-vnet-access \
  --allow-forwarded-traffic \
  --allow-gateway-transit
```

Pros:

- Low latency, high throughput
- No public IPs or VPNs required

Cons:

- Flat network architecture—lacks centralized control
- No built-in transit routing; must use UDRs or NVA

---

2. Virtual WAN

Virtual WAN simplifies complex global topologies by acting as a network transit hub with integrated routing and security.

- Centralized control of branch and Azure site connectivity

- Built-in VPN and ExpressRoute support
- Automated route propagation

```
az network vwan create \
  --name GlobalWAN \
  --resource-group NetworkRG \
  --location eastus
```

Use Cases:

- Hub-and-spoke architecture across continents
- Multi-site hybrid connectivity
- Secure global transit without manual peering

---

3. ExpressRoute Global Reach

Allows private peering between ExpressRoute circuits in different locations.

Scenario:

- Data center in US connects to Azure East US
- Data center in EU connects to Azure West Europe
- Global Reach allows on-prem sites to talk over Azure's backbone

Use Cases:

- Interconnect global on-prem data centers without MPLS
- Build a resilient multi-national backbone

DNS and Global Routing Strategies

Global applications rely heavily on DNS for directing users to the closest or healthiest endpoint.

Azure Traffic Manager

DNS-based global traffic routing based on:

- Performance   (lowest   latency)

- Priority   (failover)

- Geographic   (region-based   compliance)

- Weighted   (load   distribution)

Create a Traffic Manager profile:

```
az network traffic-manager profile create \
  --name GlobalRouting \
  --resource-group GlobalRG \
  --routing-method Performance \
  --unique-dns-name myglobalapp \
  --ttl 30 \
  --monitor-path "/" \
  --monitor-port 80 \
  --monitor-protocol HTTP
```

Add endpoints for each region (Azure App Service, Public IP, External):

```
az network traffic-manager endpoint create \
  --name EastUS \
  --profile-name GlobalRouting \
  --type azureEndpoints \
  --target-resource-id <resource-id>
```

Azure Front Door

An application-layer global load balancer with anycast routing, TLS termination, WAF, and URL-based routing.

Advantages over Traffic Manager:

- Layer   7   routing

- Caching   and   compression

- Session   affinity

- Real-time   failover   (faster   than   DNS   TTL)

Use Cases:

- Multi-region   web   applications

- Global   APIs

- SaaS   platforms   with   regional   entry   points

Data Architecture Considerations

Network design is only part of the picture—data replication and consistency must align with the network strategy.

Data Service	Multi-region Option
Azure SQL	Active Geo-Replication (manual failover)
Cosmos DB	Multi-region writes, automatic failover
Blob Storage	GRS and RA-GRS for read access from secondaries
Key Vault	Vault replication and soft delete in multiple regions
Azure Files	Geo-redundant storage with cross-region sync

Design for either:

- **Active-Active**: All regions can serve and write (e.g., Cosmos DB)

- **Active-Passive**: One region handles traffic, others standby (e.g., SQL with Geo-DR)

Secure Multi-region Design

Secure connectivity across global regions includes:

1. **Private Link + Private DNS Zones**
   Extend secure access to PaaS across regions using zonal links.

2. **Centralized Security Services**
   Deploy Azure Firewall, NVA, and Azure Bastion in each region.

3. **Custom Route Tables and NSGs**
   Apply policies to enforce traffic control and isolation across regional boundaries.

4. **Policy Enforcement**
   Use Azure Policy to restrict where resources can be deployed and ensure consistent tagging and logging.

Monitoring a Global Network

Use centralized logging with **Azure Monitor** and **Log Analytics** workspaces deployed in a region with high availability.

Monitor:

- Traffic flow between regions (Network Watcher)

- DNS latency and resolution issues (Traffic Manager Logs)

- Front Door backend health and failover events

- Bandwidth costs and traffic anomalies

Sample Kusto query to detect inter-region egress spikes:

```
AzureDiagnostics
| where ResourceType == "NETWORKINTERFACE"
| where Category == "NetworkSecurityGroupFlowEvent"
| where Direction_s == "Outbound"
| summarize bytesTransferred = sum(BytesSent_d) by Region_s,
bin(TimeGenerated, 1h)
| where bytesTransferred > 1000000000
```

High-level Multi-region Design Patterns

Pattern 1: Active/Passive DR

- Traffic Manager directs to primary
- Secondary region is warm or cold standby
- DR test run monthly with automated scripts

Pattern 2: Active/Active Global

- Azure Front Door or Traffic Manager distributes load
- Databases use Cosmos DB or SQL Geo-Replication
- Stateful traffic is avoided or synchronized

Pattern 3: Region-specific Tenants

- SaaS platform with isolated environments per geography
- Regulatory boundaries respected by DNS-based routing
- Separate network policies and keys per region

Best Practices

1. **Use Azure Front Door or Traffic Manager for global routing**
2. **Design for DNS failover and monitoring** to detect latency or outages
3. **Use paired regions for all critical resources**
4. **Plan for regulatory compliance** with geographic restrictions
5. **Minimize cross-region data flow** unless required
6. **Automate replication and failover testing**
7. **Enforce consistent network and security policy via Azure Policy**
8. **Integrate all regions into unified monitoring and alerting**
9. **Document regional boundaries and dependencies**
10. **Simulate regional failures regularly using Chaos Studio**

Summary

Global network architecture in Azure requires careful planning and deep integration between routing, security, application services, and data layers. Whether your organization is enabling local access for users worldwide or building disaster-resilient platforms, Azure provides the tools to scale and protect applications across regions and continents.

By combining services like Global VNet Peering, Virtual WAN, Front Door, Traffic Manager, and region-paired resources, you can create a seamless, high-performance, and regulatory-compliant global presence.

In the next section, we'll dive into **scalability patterns and auto-scaling strategies** that ensure your network can dynamically respond to load without sacrificing reliability or cost control.

Scalability Patterns and Auto-scaling Strategies

Scalability is a foundational design goal for any cloud-native network architecture. It ensures that systems can efficiently handle growth—in user demand, traffic volume, services, and geographic footprint—without sacrificing performance, reliability, or cost control. In Azure, scalability is achieved through both horizontal and vertical scaling strategies, the use of elastic resources, and the automation of scaling operations using native tools.

This section provides an in-depth guide to scalable network design patterns, auto-scaling capabilities across networking components, and architecture strategies for responsive, resilient, and high-throughput systems.

Scalability Dimensions in Azure Networking

Scalability can be considered along several dimensions:

Dimension	Examples
Traffic Volume	Increasing connections, throughput, requests per second
Geographic Reach	Expanding to new regions, edge locations
User Load	Handling more simultaneous users or sessions
Service Footprint	Deploying more services, APIs, endpoints

To support these, you must architect networks that can elastically scale **compute**, **routing**, **security**, and **application delivery** layers.

Core Network Components with Scalability Features

Component	Scalability Features
Azure Load Balancer	Automatic backend scaling with VMSS; supports millions of flows
Application Gateway	Autoscaling in v2 SKU; scales based on HTTP traffic patterns
Azure Firewall	Autoscale capacity and throughput; policy-based scalability
Virtual Network	Supports many subnets and large address spaces
Virtual WAN	Scales branches and endpoints dynamically
ExpressRoute	Configurable circuits up to 100 Gbps
Private Link	Supports thousands of connections across tenants

Each of these components can be designed to scale independently or in concert with application scaling strategies.

Horizontal vs Vertical Scaling

- **Horizontal scaling** (scale-out): Add more instances or resources (e.g., VMs behind a Load Balancer)

- **Vertical scaling** (scale-up): Increase the capacity (e.g., move from VpnGw1 to VpnGw3)

Horizontal scaling is preferred for most networking workloads because it:

- Reduces risk of single point failure

- Allows rolling updates

- Supports elastic architectures (autoscaling)

Autoscaling with Application Gateway and VMSS

Azure Application Gateway v2

Supports autoscaling based on HTTP traffic volume:

- Automatically increases or decreases instances

- No manual configuration required

- Supports WAF and path-based routing

Example Bicep configuration snippet for autoscale:

```
resource appGateway 'Microsoft.Network/applicationGateways@2021-03-01' = {
  name: 'myAppGateway'
  location: location
  sku: {
    name: 'WAF_v2'
    tier: 'WAF_v2'
  }
  properties: {
    autoscaleConfiguration: {
      minCapacity: 2
      maxCapacity: 10
    }
  }
}
```

Virtual Machine Scale Sets (VMSS)

Used with Load Balancer or Application Gateway to provide backend elasticity.

Autoscale triggers:

- CPU utilization

- Memory usage (via custom metrics)

- Queue   length

- Custom   Azure   Monitor   metrics

```
az monitor autoscale create \
  --resource-group MyResourceGroup \
  --resource MyScaleSet \
  --resource-type Microsoft.Compute/virtualMachineScaleSets \
  --name autoscaleProfile \
  --min-count 2 \
  --max-count 10 \
  --count 3
```

Add scale-out rule (e.g., when CPU > 70%):

```
az monitor autoscale rule create \
  --resource-group MyResourceGroup \
  --autoscale-name autoscaleProfile \
  --condition "Percentage CPU > 70 avg 5m" \
  --scale out 1
```

Scaling Azure Firewall

Azure Firewall can be deployed with automatic scaling using the **Azure Firewall Premium or Standard SKU**:

- Autoscale   adjusts   firewall   throughput   units   (FTUs)   based   on   load

- You   can   configure   min   and   max   limits

- Supports   up   to   30   Gbps   in   Standard   and   more   in   Premium

```
az network firewall create \
  --name MyFirewall \
  --resource-group MyResourceGroup \
  --sku AZFW_Hub \
  --tier Premium \
  --location eastus \
  --threat-intel-mode Alert
```

Use in conjunction with route tables and availability zones for highly scalable traffic inspection.

Scaling Out DNS and Traffic Management

Azure DNS

- Automatically scales to support billions of DNS queries
- Low-latency resolution from Azure's global DNS infrastructure

Use **alias records** and integrate with **Traffic Manager** or **Front Door** for elastic, location-aware routing.

Azure Traffic Manager

- DNS-based global load balancing
- Supports performance-based routing to scale based on latency
- No limit on the number of endpoints or profiles

Azure Front Door

- Scales automatically with demand
- Uses Anycast to route users to the closest point of presence
- Handles TLS offloading, caching, and WAF at edge

Microsegmentation and Service Scalability

Use subnet and NSG scaling patterns to support microservice and multi-tenant environments:

- **Create dedicated subnets per service tier** for isolation
- **Apply NSGs per subnet or per NIC** for granular control
- **Use Application Security Groups (ASGs)** to group and scale VM-based services logically

NSGs and ASGs scale automatically without manual reconfiguration as long as the correct rules are applied.

Network Design Patterns for Scaling

Pattern 1: Scale-out Load Balancer with VMSS

- Frontend: Azure Load Balancer
- Backend: Virtual Machine Scale Sets
- Health probes trigger instance addition/removal

Pattern 2: Autoscaling Application Gateway

- Frontend: Public IP
- Gateway: App Gateway with WAF and autoscale
- Backend: App Service or AKS with autoscale

Pattern 3: Centralized Hub Scaling with Firewall

- Hub contains Azure Firewall
- Spokes scale independently
- Route UDRs and diagnostics scale automatically

Monitoring and Auto-remediation

Use **Azure Monitor**, **Log Analytics**, and **Alerts** to automate responses to traffic spikes:

1. **Create custom metrics** for bandwidth or connection count
2. **Set thresholds and rules** for autoscaling triggers
3. **Integrate with Logic Apps** to perform advanced remediation
4. **Use Autoscale history** to tune scale parameters over time

Sample Kusto query for monitoring TCP connections per NSG:

```
AzureDiagnostics
| where Category == "NetworkSecurityGroupFlowEvent"
| where Protocol_s == "T"
| summarize Connections = count() by bin(TimeGenerated, 5m), Subnet_s
```

Challenges and Considerations

1. **Scaling** **Latency**
   Some services may take time to provision new capacity—plan accordingly.

2. **Cold** **Starts**
   Services that auto-provision may delay the first few connections.

3. **Quota** **Limits**
   Ensure resource limits (e.g., public IPs, VNets, gateways) are increased in advance.

4. **Cost** **Implications**
   Autoscaling adds cost when scaling out. Balance performance vs. budget.

5. **Stateful** **Services**
   Must be designed with session persistence or external state stores.

6. **Monitoring** **Accuracy**
   Poor metric choices lead to ineffective scaling.

Best Practices

1. **Use autoscaling wherever supported** (App Gateway, VMSS, Firewall)

2. **Align scaling to observable metrics** such as CPU, latency, or queue length

3. **Apply decoupled architectures** to allow independent service scaling

4. **Set reasonable min/max bounds** to avoid excessive cost or underperformance

5. **Monitor scale events** and adjust policies based on trends

6. **Use tags** to classify and track scalable network resources

7. **Use service-level agreements (SLAs)** to validate scaling effectiveness

8. **Test under simulated load** before production rollout

9. **Log all scaling actions** for audit and optimization

10. **Document scaling logic** and thresholds as part of your network design docs

Summary

Scalability is not a one-time task—it's a continuous design principle that ensures Azure networks can meet the dynamic demands of modern workloads. By using autoscale features, modular design patterns, and integrated observability, you can create self-adaptive network architectures that grow with your users and services.

From backend VM pools to frontend gateways, Azure offers a flexible, programmable approach to elastic infrastructure. In the next section, we'll cover performance tuning techniques and latency optimization across regional and global network designs to ensure that scalability doesn't come at the cost of responsiveness.

Performance Tuning and Latency Optimization

High-performance networking is critical for delivering responsive applications, maintaining user satisfaction, and ensuring service-level agreement (SLA) compliance. In distributed and cloud-native environments, even small latency variations can lead to significant differences in application behavior, data synchronization, and customer experience.

Azure provides a comprehensive set of tools and architectural patterns to measure, tune, and optimize network performance. This section will explore latency contributors, performance tuning techniques, low-latency design strategies, and best practices for minimizing jitter, packet loss, and bandwidth constraints—across both regional and global Azure deployments.

Key Metrics for Network Performance

To effectively optimize performance, it is essential to monitor and understand the following metrics:

Metric	Description
Latency	Time taken for a packet to travel from source to destination

Jitter	Variability in packet delay over time
Throughput	Volume of data successfully transmitted per unit of time
Packet Loss	Percentage of packets lost during transmission
Round-Trip Time	Time for a packet to reach a destination and return
Bandwidth	Maximum transfer capacity of the network path

These metrics help diagnose network bottlenecks and validate optimization efforts.

Azure Tools for Network Performance Analysis

Network   Watcher   Connection   Monitor
Continuously tests connectivity and provides insights into packet loss, RTT, and availability.

```
az network watcher connection-monitor create \
  --name MyConnectionTest \
  --resource-group MyResourceGroup \
  --location eastus \
  --source-resource MyVM \
  --dest-address contoso.com \
  --dest-port 443
```

1.
2. **Azure   Monitor   and   Log   Analytics**
   Collect performance data from VMs, gateways, firewalls, and applications.

Packet   Capture
Capture traffic at the NIC level to analyze protocol behavior and detect anomalies.

```
az network watcher packet-capture create \
  --resource-group MyResourceGroup \
  --vm-name MyVM \
  --name PerformanceCapture \
  --storage-account mystorageaccount \
  --duration 300
```

3.

4. **Application** **Gateway** **Logs**
Provide end-to-end visibility into HTTP request latency and backend health.

5. **Azure** **Front** **Door** **Metrics**
Track global edge routing performance, TLS negotiation time, and backend latency.

Regional Network Performance Tuning

1. Optimize VNet Design

- **Minimize subnet traversal**: Keep latency-sensitive resources in the same subnet when possible.

Use accelerated networking on supported VM sizes to reduce virtualization overhead and lower jitter.

```
az network nic create \
  --resource-group MyRG \
  --name MyNIC \
  --vnet-name MyVNet \
  --subnet MySubnet \
  --accelerated-networking true
```

-
- **Enable RSS (Receive Side Scaling)** to improve throughput on multi-core VMs.

2. Use Premium Network Features

- Deploy workloads on **Premium SSD** or **Ultra SSD** to reduce IOPS latency.

- Use **Standard or Premium public IPs** with Load Balancer to benefit from better SLA and throughput.

3. Tune Application Gateway

- Set appropriate **connection timeouts** and **cookie affinity** to reduce session churn.

Use **HTTP/2** for latency-sensitive traffic.

Example configuration for enabling HTTP/2:

```
az network application-gateway update \
  --name MyAppGateway \
  --resource-group MyRG \
  --enable-http2 true
```

-

Global Performance Optimization

1. Use Azure Front Door for Global Acceleration

Azure Front Door provides:

- Anycast routing: Routes users to the nearest edge node

- TLS offloading: Reduces backend CPU load

- Caching: Improves response time for static content

This drastically reduces **first byte latency** for end users globally.

2. Leverage Azure CDN

Azure CDN (Standard or Premium) caches content at edge locations, reducing round-trip times.

Use it to offload image, script, and media content and prevent data center congestion.

3. Design for Data Locality

- Keep data close to where it is consumed

- Deploy **Cosmos DB** with multi-region writes for low-latency, geo-distributed data access

- Use **Azure SQL Active Geo-Replication** to route queries to the nearest secondary

---

Reducing Cross-Region Latency

Latency between regions can vary dramatically. Reduce it by:

- Using **paired regions** to ensure optimal replication paths
- Avoiding unnecessary **data egress** by keeping traffic within region
- Using **Private Link** instead of public endpoints to access PaaS services privately
- Deploying **Virtual WAN** to centralize and optimize routing between regions

Example: Connect West Europe and North Europe via Global VNet Peering

```
az network vnet peering create \
  --name PeerWtoN \
  --resource-group RG-WEU \
  --vnet-name VNet-WEU \
  --remote-vnet VNet-NEU \
  --allow-vnet-access
```

Application-level Optimization

Network performance is not just about infrastructure. Application behavior significantly impacts perceived latency.

1. Reduce Chattiness

- Minimize API calls that require multiple round trips
- Combine or batch operations

2. Compress Payloads

- Use gzip or Brotli compression for web responses
- Avoid uncompressed image and JSON payloads

3. Optimize TLS Negotiation

- Reuse sessions
- Avoid certificate chains with unnecessary intermediates

4. Use Connection Pooling

- Avoid repeated TCP handshakes and TLS negotiations
- Ensure services use persistent or pooled connections

Measuring and Monitoring Performance

Set up performance monitoring dashboards using **Azure Monitor Workbooks**:

- Show RTT by region
- Detect latency spikes over time
- Visualize impact of scale events on throughput

Example Kusto query for RTT:

```
AzureDiagnostics
| where ResourceType == "CONNECTIONMONITORS"
| project TimeGenerated, avgRoundTripTimeMs_s, Source, Destination
| summarize avg(avgRoundTripTimeMs_s) by bin(TimeGenerated, 5m),
Destination
```

Use **alert rules** to notify teams when performance thresholds are exceeded.

Real-world Scenarios

Scenario 1: Global API with Regional Front Doors

- Use Front Door profiles per continent
- Route to nearest region backend using performance routing
- Terminate TLS at the edge
- Backend VMs use accelerated networking

Scenario 2: Data Analytics with Cross-region Storage

- Minimize data transfer using Azure Data Lake zonal availability

- Enable caching in Azure Synapse
- Use ExpressRoute for deterministic latency from on-prem pipelines

---

Best Practices

1. **Always use accelerated networking** for VM workloads
2. **Use Azure Front Door and CDN** for edge-optimized content
3. **Monitor performance with Connection Monitor and Log Analytics**
4. **Prefer paired regions and intra-region architectures**
5. **Avoid chatty protocols**—optimize payload size and frequency
6. **Deploy health probes** to detect latency at the app layer
7. **Simulate traffic and perform load testing regularly**
8. **Choose compute SKUs with sufficient NIC bandwidth**
9. **Avoid public internet where possible**—use ExpressRoute or Private Link
10. **Analyze packet captures** for real-time protocol-level bottlenecks

---

Summary

Achieving low-latency, high-throughput, and resilient network performance in Azure requires a combination of architectural planning, platform features, and continuous monitoring. From deploying edge-optimized services like Azure Front Door and CDN to fine-tuning regional configurations with accelerated networking and intelligent routing, Azure provides the tools needed to deliver premium networking performance.

As workloads scale and users become increasingly global, performance tuning becomes an ongoing discipline—essential to business success. In the next chapter, we will explore real-world scenarios and case studies that apply these principles in enterprise, government, and SaaS applications at scale.

Chapter 8: Real-World Scenarios and Case Studies

Enterprise Cloud Migration with Secure Networking

Migrating enterprise workloads to the cloud is not a matter of simply "lifting and shifting" virtual machines. It requires a detailed, deliberate approach to **network architecture**, **security**, **compliance**, **operational continuity**, and **performance**. For enterprises with legacy systems, strict regulatory requirements, and multi-region operations, secure networking is a linchpin of a successful migration strategy.

This section presents a real-world end-to-end scenario of a large enterprise migrating its on-premises datacenter to Azure. It focuses on designing and implementing a **secure, hybrid network**, transitioning to a **cloud-native topology**, and addressing operational challenges such as segmentation, access control, encryption, and observability.

Organization Background

Company: Contoso Insurance Group
Industry: Financial Services
Global Presence: HQ in London, regional offices across EU and US
Challenge: Legacy data centers nearing capacity and hardware end-of-life. Business requires agility for new digital services and disaster recovery resilience.

Key Requirements:

- Ensure zero data loss during migration

- Maintain compliance with GDPR, PCI-DSS, and local financial regulations

- Implement hybrid connectivity with low-latency performance

- Support centralized security inspection and policy enforcement

- Achieve regional high availability and long-term scalability

---

Phase 1: Hybrid Foundation with VPN and ExpressRoute

Objective

Establish secure connectivity between Azure and the on-premises data centers to allow phased migration, replication, and DR testing.

Design

- Deploy **hub-and-spoke network topology** with centralized inspection
- Establish **site-to-site VPN** for immediate connectivity
- Provision **ExpressRoute circuit** for high-throughput and SLA-backed redundancy
- Integrate on-prem DNS with Azure Private DNS

Implementation

Hub VNet contains:

- Azure Firewall Premium (centralized inspection)
- Azure Bastion (remote management)
- Log Analytics workspace
- Shared services (Jump box, monitoring agents)

Spoke VNets:

- Separated per business domain: Claims, Underwriting, CustomerPortal
- Connected via VNet peering to the hub

Connectivity Setup:

```
az network vpn-gateway create \
  --name ContosoVPNGW \
  --public-ip-address ContosoVPNGWIP \
  --resource-group NetworkRG \
  --vnet ContosoHubVNet \
  --gateway-type Vpn \
  --vpn-type RouteBased \
  --sku VpnGw2
```

ExpressRoute was enabled with **Private Peering** and integrated into the same hub for redundancy.

Phase 2: Secure Access Control and Segmentation

Objective

Segment traffic between departments and enforce zero-trust access principles.

Techniques Used

1. **Network Security Groups (NSGs)** for subnet-level restrictions

2. **Application Security Groups (ASGs)** to manage rules by workload tag

3. **User Defined Routes (UDRs)** to force all outbound traffic through Azure Firewall

4. **Private Link** for access to Azure SQL and Blob Storage

Example UDR for forced tunneling:

```
az network route-table route create \
  --resource-group NetworkRG \
  --route-table-name SpokeRouteTable \
  --name ToFirewall \
  --address-prefix 0.0.0.0/0 \
  --next-hop-type VirtualAppliance \
  --next-hop-ip-address 10.1.1.4
```

Each spoke had its own NSG and route table, linked to the appropriate subnet.

Private DNS zones were created for `privatelink.database.windows.net` and `privatelink.blob.core.windows.net`, and linked to the VNet.

Phase 3: Application Migration and Network Scaling

Objective

Lift and shift tiered applications with minimal downtime, while introducing cloud-native enhancements.

Workloads Migrated

- Customer portal (web + API + backend DB)

- Claims processing service (batch workload with file storage)
- Internal CRM and reporting (legacy apps)

Migration Strategy:

- Use **Azure** **Migrate** to assess and rehost VMs
- Modernize backend using Azure SQL Managed Instance
- Use **VM Scale Sets** and **Application Gateway WAF** for front-end scaling
- Deploy multiple Availability Zones for high availability

Application Gateway Setup with Autoscale:

```
az network application-gateway create \
  --name AppGatewayClaims \
  --location westeurope \
  --resource-group ClaimsRG \
  --sku WAF_v2 \
  --capacity 2 \
  --frontend-port 443 \
  --vnet-name ClaimsVNet \
  --subnet SubnetAG \
  --http-settings-cookie-based-affinity Enabled
```

Phase 4: Monitoring, Logging, and Compliance

Objective

Enable centralized monitoring and logging to support operational visibility and regulatory compliance.

Tools and Techniques

- **Azure** **Monitor** for metrics and alerts
- **Log** **Analytics** for traffic inspection, flow logs, and diagnostics
- **Azure** **Policy** to enforce network configuration standards

- **Azure Sentinel** for SIEM and threat detection

Diagnostic Settings Example for Firewall Logs:

```
az monitor diagnostic-settings create \
  --resource
/subscriptions/<subId>/resourceGroups/NetworkRG/providers/Microsoft.
Network/azureFirewalls/ContosoFirewall \
  --workspace ContosoLogAnalytics \
  --name FirewallDiagnostics \
  --logs  '[{"category":  "AzureFirewallNetworkRule",  "enabled":
true}]'
```

Azure Policy initiatives enforced:

- Mandatory NSGs on all subnets
- Prohibit public IPs on VM NICs
- Required tagging for all networking components
- Logging enabled on all gateways and firewalls

Phase 5: Business Continuity and Disaster Recovery

Objective

Ensure failover to a secondary region in case of a regional outage.

Strategy

- Active/passive regional deployment (West Europe ↔ North Europe)
- Data replication via Geo-Replication (Blob, SQL MI)
- Traffic Manager for failover routing

Traffic Manager Profile Setup:

```
az network traffic-manager profile create \
  --name ContosoDRRouting \
```

```
--resource-group GlobalRG \
--routing-method Priority \
--unique-dns-name contosoapp \
--monitor-path "/" \
--monitor-port 443 \
--monitor-protocol HTTPS
```

Endpoints:

- West   Europe   (Priority   1)

- North   Europe   (Priority   2)

Failover was tested quarterly using live drills with success criteria.

Results and Outcomes

- All   workloads   successfully   migrated   within   8   months

- Zero   critical   incidents   during   or   after   cutover

- Reduced   datacenter   operating   cost   by   ~42%

- Achieved   full   compliance   with   financial   regulations   and   audit   logs

- Improved   customer   portal   response   times   globally   using   Azure   Front   Door

- Network   traffic   encrypted   end-to-end   and   monitored   continuously

- Able   to   scale   application   capacity   10x   during   seasonal   demand

---

Lessons Learned

1. **Start   with   network   and   identity** before   touching   apps

2. **Use   Azure   Migrate   for   phased   and   controlled   transitions**

3. **Automate   everything** with   Bicep   and   Azure   DevOps   pipelines

4. **Tag   everything** from   day   one—critical   for   billing   and   compliance

5. **Engage security teams early** to define policies, not just validate them

6. **Use Policy as Code** to enforce consistent governance

7. **Test DR scenarios early**—assumptions don't guarantee resilience

8. **Centralize firewalling and diagnostics** to simplify operations

Summary

Enterprise cloud migration is a complex but achievable goal with the right planning and tooling. In the Contoso Insurance case, a robust hybrid foundation, segmentation strategy, automated governance, and resilient global network design enabled a seamless transition from legacy infrastructure to modern, scalable Azure environments. Secure networking wasn't an afterthought—it was the bedrock upon which the migration succeeded.

In the next section, we'll explore how SaaS providers design multi-tenant, internet-facing applications on Azure using secure, scalable, and cost-effective networking architectures.

SaaS Application Deployment in Azure

Software as a Service (SaaS) has become the dominant model for delivering scalable, on-demand, subscription-based software applications. Azure offers a wide range of capabilities and patterns to support the deployment of SaaS solutions—from multi-tenant isolation to global delivery, zero-trust networking, and automated scaling.

In this section, we examine the networking architecture and deployment strategies of a fictional SaaS company, **Syntara**, building a productivity platform serving customers worldwide. The case study walks through every phase—from initial architecture to scaling, cost control, compliance, and observability—highlighting decisions, trade-offs, and best practices relevant to real SaaS deployments.

Business Requirements

Company: Syntara Inc.
Industry: Technology / Productivity SaaS
Customers: Small to mid-sized businesses in North America and Europe
Key Drivers:

- Multi-tenant design with strict data isolation

- Elastic, globally accessible infrastructure

- Integrated zero-trust security and access control

- High availability and low latency

- Metered usage tracking and cost allocation

Core Network Architecture

Multi-Tier SaaS Layout

Syntara adopted a **hub-and-spoke** VNet topology enhanced with **multi-region deployments** and **network segmentation**.

- **Hub VNet**: Central services (logging, monitoring, DNS, Bastion, Azure Firewall)

- **Spoke VNet (per environment)**: Dedicated for staging, dev, and production

- **Per-Tenant Isolation**: Tenants grouped logically by subscription and spoke VNet

- **Ingress Layer**: Azure Front Door + Application Gateway

- **Egress Filtering**: Azure Firewall and NSG/UDR enforcement

Each tenant's workloads were containerized (via AKS) or deployed via Azure App Services depending on complexity and scale.

Ingress and Load Balancing Strategy

Azure Front Door

Used as the global entry point with features such as:

- Anycast-based routing to the closest region

- TLS offloading and certificate management

- WAF integration for OWASP protection

- URL path-based routing

Multi-region configuration:

```
az network front-door create \
  --name SyntaraFrontDoor \
  --resource-group GlobalRG \
  --backend-pool default \
  --accepted-protocols Http Https \
  --backend-hostname tenantportal.syntara.com
```

Application Gateway

Used for region-specific routing and connection termination to Azure App Services or AKS workloads.

- Configured with autoscaling (v2 SKU)

- Internal App Gateway used for tenant-to-tenant microservices communication

- WAF policy applied for L7 security

Multi-Tenancy Patterns

Option 1: Shared App Infrastructure

- Single App Service Plan, shared by multiple tenants

- Tenant ID passed in JWT token or HTTP header

- Common database with row-level security or per-tenant schema

Pros:

- Lower cost

- Simpler scaling

Cons:

- Harder to guarantee strong isolation

Option 2: Isolated App Infrastructure (Preferred for High-Value Tenants)

- Dedicated App Services or AKS namespace per tenant

- Optional isolated VNets or subnet per tenant

- Managed Identity per tenant

Pros:

- Stronger security and compliance

- Granular cost attribution and scaling

Syntara used a **hybrid model**, offering shared infrastructure to SMBs and isolated deployments to enterprise customers.

Secure Access with Azure AD B2C and Private Link

Syntara's authentication was handled via **Azure AD B2C**, enabling social and enterprise login for end users. Management APIs and backend services used **Azure AD App Registrations** with RBAC and PIM controls.

API Gateway Access

- APIs deployed to Azure API Management (APIM)

- Private endpoint added to APIM for internal service access

- Azure Application Gateway used for external access to APIs

Example: Creating Private Endpoint for APIM

```
az network private-endpoint create \
  --name APIMPrivateEndpoint \
  --resource-group CoreServices \
  --vnet-name CoreVNet \
  --subnet APIMSubnet \
  --private-connection-resource-id <apim-resource-id> \
  --group-id gateway
```

Private DNS zone linked to CoreVNet to resolve APIM's internal hostname.

Database and Storage Architecture

Syntara required both strong tenant-level isolation and high availability for stateful services.

- Azure SQL Database: per-tenant logical database or elastic pool
- Cosmos DB: for low-latency metadata and user activity logs
- Blob Storage: tenant-specific containers with private endpoint access
- Redis Cache: shared across tenants with tenant-aware key prefixes

Storage and database services were integrated with **Private Link** and **NSGs** to prevent public access.

Observability and Metering

Monitoring was centralized through **Log Analytics** and **Azure Monitor**.

- **Custom dashboards** for per-tenant metrics (via tags)
- **App Insights** for request traces, dependencies, and performance
- **Azure Monitor Metrics** for API usage, latency, and error rates

Usage tracking was achieved via:

- Telemetry headers on all HTTP traffic
- Logging per-tenant metrics to dedicated workspaces
- Billing system integrated with Azure Cost Management + tagging

Sample metric aggregation query:

```
AppRequests
| where cloud_RoleName startswith "tenant-"
| summarize requests = count() by tenantId =
customDimensions.tenantId, bin(timestamp, 1h)
```

High Availability and Scalability Design

1. **Region Pairing**: West Europe ↔ North Europe, East US ↔ Central US

2. **AKS** **with** **Horizontal** **Pod** **Autoscaler**

3. **Auto-scale** **rules** **for** **App** **Services** **and** **Cosmos** **DB** **throughput**

4. **Global** **Traffic** **Manager** **fallback** **for** **API** **availability**

5. **Azure** **Load** **Testing** before major releases

Scaling rules:

```
az monitor autoscale create \
  --resource-group SyntaraProd \
  --resource syntara-web-app \
  --resource-type Microsoft.Web/sites \
  --name scaleAppService \
  --min-count 3 \
  --max-count 15
```

Cost Control and Optimization

- Tenant resources tagged with TenantId, Environment, and CostCenter

- Policy preventing use of Premium SKUs unless approved

- Scheduled scale-in scripts for off-peak hours

- Alert thresholds for over-utilization or cost anomalies

Sample Policy: Deny Premium SKUs for Shared Tier

```
{
  "if": {
    "allOf": [
      { "field": "Microsoft.Web/serverfarms/sku.name", "equals":
"P1v2" },
      { "field": "tags.Tier", "equals": "Shared" }
    ]
  },
  "then": {
```

```
      "effect": "deny"
    }
}
```

Security and Compliance

- **WAF** **with** **custom** **rules** for API and web ingress
- **Private** **endpoints** for all data services
- **Key** **Vault** **with** **RBAC** **+** **Private** **Link**
- **Azure** **Defender** **for** **Cloud** enabled on all subscriptions
- **Azure** **Policy** **Initiatives** for GDPR, ISO27001 baseline enforcement

Quarterly **penetration testing** and monthly **DR simulations** were part of the standard operating procedure.

Summary

Deploying SaaS applications on Azure at scale requires a carefully architected network, security-first mindset, automation, and tenant-aware resource governance. Syntara's approach—built on a hub-and-spoke architecture with hybrid tenancy, centralized policy enforcement, and global ingress/egress optimization—enabled it to serve thousands of customers securely and efficiently.

The success of a SaaS platform on Azure depends not just on code, but on the surrounding network fabric that supports secure access, global performance, operational transparency, and cost efficiency. In the next section, we'll examine a high-security government cloud deployment with even stricter compliance and isolation requirements.

High-Security Government Cloud Implementation

Government agencies operate under some of the strictest security, compliance, and operational control requirements in the world. They must protect sensitive citizen data, ensure system availability during national emergencies, and meet highly specific regulatory frameworks such as FedRAMP High, CJIS, ITAR, and NIST 800-53. Azure Government Cloud and Microsoft's Sovereign Cloud offerings provide a secure platform purpose-built for public sector workloads.

In this section, we explore a high-security implementation scenario for a fictional national government agency, **GovSecure**, tasked with modernizing its infrastructure for mission-critical applications across multiple departments. The project highlights real-world network architecture principles, compliance strategies, isolation techniques, and secure connectivity patterns required in sensitive government environments.

Background and Requirements

Agency: GovSecure National Services
Scope: National identity, benefits, and citizen services
Current Infrastructure: On-premises private data centers with air-gapped segments
Drivers for Migration:

- End of life on hardware and software

- Cost pressure and operational complexity

- Need for global threat intelligence integration

- Legislative mandate for digital-first services

Key Security Requirements:

- End-to-end encryption

- Segmented, zero-trust network

- Strict workload isolation per agency

- Multi-level access control (user, device, role, location)

- Continuous monitoring and audit logging

- All traffic inspected through central firewall/NVA

- Use of only FedRAMP High certified services

Azure Government Cloud Strategy

GovSecure chose **Azure Government (USGov)** for its FedRAMP High coverage and geographic availability across physically isolated data centers. Azure Government provides:

- Network separation from commercial Azure
- Compliance with ITAR, DoD IL5, and CJIS
- Regional availability for failover and HA
- Support for hybrid and disconnected operations

Resource provisioning and access were done via **separate Azure Active Directory tenants** tied to **Azure AD Government** identity services.

Network Architecture Overview

GovSecure adopted a **hub-and-spoke** model with **dedicated regional zones** and **multi-layered segmentation**:

- **National Hub VNet** (per region): Hosts shared services like Azure Firewall, Bastion, DNS, and Private Link endpoints.

- **Agency Spokes**: Each department (Health, Tax, Welfare) has its own VNet, subscription, and policy boundary.

- **Policy Enforced Peering**: All peerings allowed only through the hub for inspection and logging.

Example: Agency Peering via Hub

```
az network vnet peering create \
  --name TaxToHub \
  --resource-group RG-Tax \
  --vnet-name VNet-Tax \
  --remote-vnet VNet-Hub \
  --allow-vnet-access \
  --allow-forwarded-traffic false
```

Inter-agency traffic was denied at NSG and UDR levels unless explicitly permitted through central firewall policies.

Secure Connectivity and Isolation

Hybrid Connectivity

Each on-premises site connected via:

- **ExpressRoute** **circuits** (private peering)
- **ExpressRoute** **Global** **Reach** for regional inter-datacenter routing
- **VPN** **fallback** **tunnels** for high-availability scenarios

Traffic routing:

- Forced through Azure Firewall for inspection
- Configured with **UDRs** and **BGP** **route** **tables**

Private Link and DNS Strategy

All PaaS services (Azure SQL, Key Vault, Blob Storage) were accessed **exclusively via Private Link**.

Private DNS Zones:

- `privatelink.database.usgovcloudapi.net`

- `privatelink.vaultcore.usgovcloudapi.net`

DNS resolution was centralized and managed using Azure Private DNS and conditional forwarding from on-prem DNS servers.

Application and Data Security

Azure Firewall

- Deployed in **HA** **configuration** **across** **Availability** **Zones**
- Integrated with **Threat** **Intelligence** **Mode:** **Alert** **and** **Deny**
- Configured with **application** **rulesets** to whitelist FQDNs
- DNS proxy enabled to inspect and log queries

```
az network firewall application-rule create \
  --collection-name GovServicesAllow \
  --name AllowServiceAPI \
```

```
--firewall-name GovSecureFirewall \
--resource-group RG-Hub \
--rule-type Allow \
--protocols Http=80 Https=443 \
--target-fqdns api.service.gov.us \
--source-addresses 10.10.0.0/16
```

Network Security Groups

- Enforced strict segmentation between tiers (web, app, data)

- Applied at both subnet and NIC levels

- Monitored via NSG flow logs with retention in Log Analytics

Identity and Access Controls

GovSecure applied a **zero-trust architecture** using the following:

- **Azure AD Conditional Access** policies for device, location, and role-based enforcement

- **Privileged Identity Management (PIM)** for time-bound administrative access

- **Managed Identities** for all applications—no embedded credentials

- **Access Reviews** and Just-in-Time (JIT) access using Microsoft Entra ID Governance (Azure AD)

Each department had delegated administrative access to its subscription but was governed by central policy enforcement.

Policy Enforcement and Compliance Automation

Compliance was automated using **Azure Policy** and **Management Groups**.

Initiatives applied:

- Enforce tag policy: Agency, Classification, Environment

- Deny public IPs on all resources
- Deploy diagnostic settings automatically for all network resources
- Only allow storage accounts with private endpoint configuration

Sample Policy: Deny Public Access to Key Vault

```
{
  "if": {
    "allOf": [
      { "field": "type", "equals": "Microsoft.KeyVault/vaults" },
      {                                                    "field":
"Microsoft.KeyVault/vaults/networkAcls.defaultAction",      "equals":
"Allow" }
    ]
  },
  "then": {
    "effect": "deny"
  }
}
```

Logging, SIEM, and Continuous Monitoring

Azure Sentinel (deployed in Gov US East) was configured as the **central SIEM** with:

- NSG flow logs
- Firewall logs
- Azure AD sign-ins and Conditional Access reports
- Defender for Cloud alerts
- Application Gateway diagnostics

Log retention policies were compliant with NIST 800-92 and matched internal security audit standards.

Sample Kusto Query for Inbound Anomalies:

```
AzureDiagnostics
```

```
| where Category == "AzureFirewallNetworkRule"
| where action_s == "Deny"
| summarize count() by SourceIP_s, bin(TimeGenerated, 1h)
```

High Availability and Disaster Recovery

- Redundant VNets in Gov US East and Gov US Arizona
- Load-balanced ingress via **Azure Front Door (Government SKU)**
- **Traffic Manager** with priority routing for regional DR
- DR drills executed quarterly with success metrics and rollback plans
- All data replicated using **Geo-redundant storage (RA-GRS)** with encryption

Summary of Outcomes

- Over 2,000 workloads securely migrated within 14 months
- No security incidents reported post go-live
- 100% audit compliance with national standards
- Reduced provisioning time for new applications from 12 weeks to 4 hours
- Centralized network monitoring improved MTTD by 60%
- Reusable policy-as-code reduced configuration drift
- Over 300 apps integrated with Azure AD for consistent identity governance

Key Lessons Learned

1. **Design isolation from day one**—retroactive segmentation is painful
2. **Use management groups** to apply consistent security controls
3. **Invest in Private Link and DNS strategy early** to reduce outages

4. **Automate logging and monitoring**—not just alerts, but structured insights

5. **Simplify identity** through centralized Azure AD and PIM

6. **Tag everything**—ownership, classification, and environment

7. **Audit access regularly**—human and application

8. **Design for failure**—simulate outages before they happen

Summary

Government cloud adoption demands more than just technical compliance—it requires strategic alignment of architecture, policy, and operations. GovSecure's implementation on Azure Government Cloud demonstrates how strict network segmentation, private access models, policy automation, and observability can support the transformation of legacy agencies into secure, modern, cloud-native operations.

In the next section, we'll analyze real incidents where network misconfigurations or overlooked best practices led to security or availability problems—and the lessons they provide.

Lessons from Network Security Incidents

Despite the best planning, security architecture, and tooling, network security incidents can and do occur. The goal of cloud networking design is not to eliminate all risk—which is impossible—but to minimize the blast radius, detect compromise early, and enable rapid recovery. Learning from past incidents is one of the most effective ways to build resilience into cloud network environments.

This section explores real-world lessons drawn from anonymized or representative incidents that occurred across cloud environments, particularly within Azure-based architectures. Each example includes a breakdown of what went wrong, how it was discovered, the mitigations applied, and the lessons learned. These case studies reinforce critical security concepts and emphasize proactive operational strategies.

Case Study 1: Unrestricted NSG Rule Leads to External Breach

Incident Summary

An internal test environment for a web application was deployed using a default Network Security Group (NSG) template. The NSG included a rule allowing inbound TCP traffic on ports 80, 443, and 3389 from any source IP address.

The environment was connected to the production network via VNet peering to test performance integration.

A vulnerability in the web application allowed an attacker to exploit an unpatched dependency and pivot from the web tier to access services in the production subnet.

Root Causes

- Default NSG template not reviewed before deployment

- No network segmentation between test and production

- No firewall or Azure Policy enforcement for NSG hygiene

- Missing threat detection or logging on the test subnet

Resolution

- Deployed Azure Policy to block NSGs with wildcard ($*$) source addresses

- Required approval workflows for peering requests across environments

- Integrated NSG Flow Logs with Azure Sentinel for behavioral analytics

- Rolled out automated NSG compliance scans using Azure Security Center

Lessons Learned

1. **Treat test environments as production-adjacent** if they are network-connected

2. **Never allow unrestricted inbound rules**—even temporarily

3. **Apply NSG rule review automation** during CI/CD pipelines

4. **Peering ≠ isolation**—use Azure Firewall or NVA segmentation

---

Case Study 2: Forgotten Public IP Exposes Data Collector

Incident Summary

A legacy VM used to collect telemetry data from IoT devices was deployed early in the project and assigned a Standard Public IP. When the workload moved to a PaaS service, the VM was no longer in use but remained active.

Months later, it was discovered that the IP was being scanned and exploited by a botnet. The endpoint was used as a springboard for SSH brute-force attacks on unrelated third-party infrastructure, traced back to the enterprise tenant.

Root Causes

- No automation to deallocate unused public IPs
- No tagging or resource expiration tracking
- Lack of policy to block lingering resources
- No monitoring for idle or high-risk exposed endpoints

Resolution

- Implemented scheduled cleanup jobs using Azure Automation
- Enforced Azure Policy to deny public IPs on non-prod VMs
- Required tagging with Owner, ExpiresOn, and Environment
- Enabled Microsoft Defender for Cloud to identify exposed endpoints

Lessons Learned

1. **Every public IP should be intentional and monitored**
2. **Use tagging + automation to expire old or unused resources**
3. **Idle resources still generate risk and cost**
4. **Scan and alert on external exposure weekly or continuously**

Case Study 3: Private Endpoint DNS Misconfiguration

Incident Summary

A company implemented Azure Private Link for accessing Azure SQL and Storage accounts. They created a private DNS zone and linked it to a VNet. However, a second spoke VNet was not linked to the zone, nor configured with DNS forwarding.

As a result, applications deployed in that spoke failed to resolve the endpoint, defaulting to public DNS and attempting to connect via public IP—resulting in blocked connections, failed deployments, and service downtime.

Root Causes

- Misconfigured DNS resolution for Private Link
- Lack of monitoring or alerts on DNS fallback behavior
- Manual oversight when adding new VNets

Resolution

- Created a centralized Private DNS management process
- Linked all VNets to shared DNS zones using Bicep modules
- Integrated alerts into Azure Monitor to detect failed resolutions
- Used `networkWatcher` `dns-resolution` to audit DNS behavior

```
az network watcher dns-resolve \
  --name storageaccount.privatelink.blob.core.windows.net \
  --resource-group RG \
  --dns-servers 10.0.0.4
```

Lessons Learned

1. **DNS is a critical component of Private Link deployments**
2. **Link all relevant VNets to DNS zones centrally**
3. **Always test name resolution from each subnet before go-live**
4. **Use diagnostics and queries to validate end-to-end DNS behavior**

Case Study 4: Lateral Movement via Misconfigured Route Tables

Incident Summary

An application was deployed using custom UDRs to route traffic through an NVA firewall. During expansion to a new environment, a route table was copied and reused, but without modifying the `next-hop IP`. As a result, traffic from the new subnet was routed through a different agency's firewall.

The firewall allowed internal traffic from trusted ranges, inadvertently permitting cross-agency access.

The issue went undetected for weeks until a routine audit revealed data leakage through network logs.

Root Causes

- Reused infrastructure as code (IaC) modules without parameterization
- Lack of route validation after deployment
- Missing egress filtering at subnet boundaries

Resolution

- Modularized route tables in Bicep with required parameters
- Added CI tests to verify route destination accuracy
- Enforced NSG deny rules for east-west traffic not explicitly allowed
- Used Azure Route Analytics to visualize traffic flow anomalies

Lessons Learned

1. **Route tables must be tenant- and environment-specific**
2. **Validate every route after deployment**
3. **Use NSGs to enforce layered access control—not routing alone**
4. **Visualize traffic with tools like Network Watcher and Flow Logs**

Case Study 5: Delayed Alerting on DDoS Attack

Incident Summary

An online government portal was targeted by a DDoS attack originating from a botnet. The Azure DDoS Protection Standard plan was enabled but improperly configured:

- The alerting was set up for a non-monitored email inbox
- The mitigation worked, but security teams were unaware for hours
- Application logs showed slow responses, but no correlation was made

This delay in visibility created confusion and a public incident declaration despite no data loss or compromise.

Root Causes

- Poor alert configuration and alert recipient hygiene
- No dashboard aggregation of network-layer alerts
- Missed integration between Azure DDoS and Sentinel

Resolution

- Alerts routed to Microsoft Teams and PagerDuty for 24/7 visibility
- Custom Sentinel workbook created for DDoS event history
- DDoS metrics integrated into daily NOC dashboards

Lessons Learned

1. **Enabling protection ≠ being protected—alerts must be actionable**
2. **Route alerts to live operators, not static email**
3. **Integrate Azure DDoS into SIEM and dashboards**
4. **Use incident drills to rehearse not just failure, but response**

General Recommendations

From these incidents, the following strategies can significantly reduce risk:

- **Adopt policy-as-code** to enforce NSG, IP, and route configurations

- **Use automation to detect idle or misconfigured resources**

- **Audit DNS, routing, and access paths regularly**

- **Establish tagging standards with ownership, expiration, and purpose**

- **Make alerting part of your DR and incident response design**

- **Involve security teams from the beginning of network design**

- **Treat infrastructure code as production-critical software**

Summary

Each incident described reinforces a simple truth: network security isn't just about preventing attackers—it's about preventing mistakes, detecting missteps early, and designing for failure containment. Whether the issue is an open port, misrouted subnet, or silent failure in DNS, every gap is a potential vector for exploitation or disruption.

By turning each incident into actionable improvements, organizations can evolve toward a security-first, operations-driven approach to Azure networking—resilient not just in design, but in culture and practice. In the final chapter, we'll summarize key concepts, provide learning resources, and share tools and templates to help you apply these lessons in your own environment.

Chapter 9: Appendices

Glossary of Terms

Understanding cloud networking in Azure requires familiarity with a broad and sometimes complex set of terms. This glossary compiles and explains the most commonly used concepts, acronyms, and service names referenced throughout the book. Whether you're a beginner needing clarity or an experienced professional seeking quick reference, this glossary serves as a foundational tool for learning and communication.

A

ACL   **(Access**   **Control**   **List)**
A set of rules used to control network traffic based on IP addresses, protocols, or ports. In Azure, NSGs serve a similar function.

AKS   **(Azure**   **Kubernetes**   **Service)**
A managed container orchestration service for running Kubernetes clusters in Azure. Integrated with Azure networking through VNet, load balancers, and network policies.

App   **Gateway**   **(Application**   **Gateway)**
A layer 7 (application layer) load balancer with support for SSL termination, path-based routing, and Web Application Firewall (WAF).

ASG   **(Application**   **Security**   **Group)**
An Azure construct that allows you to group virtual machine NICs together for simplified NSG rule management.

B

BGP   **(Border**   **Gateway**   **Protocol)**
A routing protocol used to exchange routing information between autonomous systems on the internet. Used in ExpressRoute and VPN Gateway configurations.

Bicep
A domain-specific language (DSL) for deploying Azure resources via Infrastructure as Code. Compiles to ARM templates and simplifies deployment.

Bastion
Azure Bastion is a PaaS service providing secure RDP and SSH access to VMs directly from the Azure portal without exposing VMs to the internet.

C

CIDR   **(Classless**   **Inter-Domain**   **Routing)**
A method for allocating IP addresses and routing. Azure VNets use CIDR blocks to define address spaces and subnets.

CDN   **(Content**   **Delivery**   **Network)**
A distributed system of servers used to deliver web content and media to users based on geographic location. Azure CDN improves global performance and reduces latency.

Connection   **Monitor**
A feature of Azure Network Watcher used to monitor network connectivity between Azure resources or between Azure and on-premises resources.

Custom   **DNS**
Custom Domain Name System configuration that allows Azure VNets to resolve names using user-defined DNS servers instead of Azure's default service.

D

DDoS   **(Distributed**   **Denial-of-Service)**
An attack that overwhelms a service with traffic. Azure DDoS Protection provides automatic detection and mitigation at the network edge.

DNS   **(Domain**   **Name**   **System)**
A service that translates domain names into IP addresses. Azure supports public DNS zones and private DNS zones for internal name resolution.

Dynamic   **Routing**
Routing where changes in the network topology automatically propagate, typically using BGP. Common in hybrid connections like ExpressRoute.

E

ExpressRoute
A private, dedicated connection between an on-premises network and Azure. Offers higher reliability, security, and lower latency compared to public internet.

Egress
Outbound data transfer from Azure to the internet or another region. Often incurs cost and should be minimized for security and budget purposes.

Endpoint
A network-accessible service or interface. In Azure, endpoints are used in private link, storage access, and web services.

F

Firewall **(Azure** **Firewall)**
A managed, cloud-based network security service that protects Azure Virtual Network resources. Includes support for application rules, logging, and threat intelligence.

Front **Door** **(Azure** **Front** **Door)**
A global entry point for high-performance, scalable, and secure delivery of web applications using Microsoft's global edge network.

Flow **Logs**
Logs that capture traffic flow information at the NSG level for auditing and monitoring. Useful for diagnosing traffic patterns and anomalies.

G

Geo-Redundancy
The distribution of services or data across multiple geographic regions to ensure high availability and disaster recovery.

Gateway
A device or service that routes traffic between different networks. Azure offers VPN Gateway and ExpressRoute Gateway.

Global **VNet** **Peering**
Allows VNets in different Azure regions to connect directly using Azure's backbone network, enabling seamless global architectures.

H

HA **(High** **Availability)**
A design principle that ensures a system remains accessible and functional during failures. In Azure, this includes redundancy across Availability Zones and regions.

Hub-and-Spoke
A network topology where the central hub VNet contains shared services and spokes represent workloads. Enhances security and simplifies traffic inspection.

I

IAAS   (Infrastructure   as   a   Service)
A cloud service model that provides virtualized computing resources over the internet. In Azure, examples include Virtual Machines and VNets.

Ingress
Inbound data traffic to Azure services or VMs. Typically monitored for security and throughput.

Initiative   (Azure   Policy)
A collection of policies grouped together to track compliance with broader standards such as CIS, ISO 27001, or internal corporate rules.

J

JIT   (Just-In-Time   Access)
A security mechanism allowing temporary access to VMs for administration, reducing attack surface. Configurable through Azure Defender.

K

Key   Vault
An Azure service used to securely store and access secrets, keys, and certificates. Integrates with Private Link for secure access over the VNet.

L

Latency
The delay before a transfer of data begins following an instruction. Azure provides tools like Front Door and Traffic Manager to reduce latency globally.

Load   Balancer
A networking service that distributes incoming network traffic across multiple servers. Azure offers both Basic and Standard SKUs for internal and external balancing.

M

Managed   Identity
A service that provides an automatically managed identity in Azure AD for applications to use when connecting to resources.

MTTR   (Mean   Time   to   Recovery)
A metric that measures the average time taken to recover from a system failure.

N

NAT   **Gateway**
A service that provides outbound internet connectivity for VMs without exposing them to direct inbound access.

NSG   **(Network**   **Security**   **Group)**
A security boundary applied at subnet or NIC level, allowing or denying traffic based on IP, port, and protocol rules.

NVA   **(Network**   **Virtual**   **Appliance)**
A virtualized network appliance, such as a third-party firewall or router, deployed in Azure for advanced traffic control.

O

Outbound   **Rules**
Rules applied to govern how outbound traffic is handled, typically configured on Load Balancers or NAT Gateways.

P

Peering
Allows VNets to communicate with each other using Azure's backbone network without requiring gateways.

Private   **Endpoint**
A network interface that connects you privately and securely to a service powered by Azure Private Link.

PIM   **(Privileged**   **Identity**   **Management)**
Azure AD feature that manages, controls, and monitors access within Azure AD, Azure, and other Microsoft Online Services.

Q

QoS   **(Quality**   **of**   **Service)**
The practice of prioritizing certain types of network traffic to ensure performance consistency.

R

RBAC   **(Role-Based**   **Access**   **Control)**
A system that restricts system access to authorized users. Azure RBAC allows fine-grained control of resource access.

Route   **Table**
A set of rules that determine how network traffic is directed. Custom routes can override default Azure routes.

S

Scalability
The ability of a system to handle increased load by scaling resources horizontally or vertically.

Service   **Endpoint**
A method to secure traffic between VNets and Azure PaaS services without requiring public IPs.

SIEM   **(Security**   **Information**   **and**   **Event**   **Management)**
A centralized system for collecting, analyzing, and acting upon security data, such as Azure Sentinel.

T

Tagging
Metadata applied to Azure resources to support cost tracking, automation, and resource organization.

Traffic   **Manager**
A DNS-based global load balancer that distributes traffic based on performance, priority, or geography.

U

UDR   **(User**   **Defined**   **Route)**
Custom route that overrides Azure's default system routes for more granular control of traffic flow.

V

VNet   **(Virtual**   **Network)**
Azure's fundamental network infrastructure allowing resource communication and segmentation.

VPN   **Gateway**
A network gateway that provides secure cross-premises connectivity via IPsec/IKE VPN tunnels.

W

WAF   **(Web**   **Application**   **Firewall)**
A security feature that protects web applications from common exploits and vulnerabilities, integrated with Application Gateway and Front Door.

Z

Zero   **Trust**
A security model that assumes breach and enforces strict verification for every access request regardless of origin.

Zones   **(Availability**   **Zones)**
Physically separated datacenters within a region offering high availability and fault isolation.

Summary

This glossary serves as a foundational reference to Azure networking terminology. Whether planning architecture, reviewing incidents, writing policy, or deploying infrastructure, understanding these core concepts enables more effective communication and execution. In the next appendix, we provide curated resources for continuous learning to help you stay current and go deeper into the topics that matter most.

Resources for Further Learning

Mastering Azure networking goes far beyond reading a single guide. Cloud networking is a dynamic field that continually evolves with new services, features, design patterns, and security requirements. Whether you're a cloud architect, network engineer, DevOps specialist, or security professional, staying current and deepening your knowledge is essential to building and maintaining scalable, secure, and high-performance cloud environments.

This section provides a curated collection of resources to extend your learning, ranging from official Microsoft documentation to advanced certifications, community content, open-source tools, and recommended hands-on labs. Use these resources to build a continuous learning plan and develop domain expertise that goes beyond theory into effective, real-world practice.

Microsoft Official Documentation

The Azure documentation is updated regularly and serves as the canonical source of truth for all Azure services.

Key Documentation Portals

- **Azure**   **Networking**   **Documentation**
  https://learn.microsoft.com/en-us/azure/networking/
  Covers core services like VNet, Load Balancer, Application Gateway, Private Link, and ExpressRoute.

- **Azure**   **Security**   **Documentation**
  https://learn.microsoft.com/en-us/azure/security/
  Includes Azure Defender, network security, policy management, and governance best practices.

- **Azure**   **Architecture**   **Center**
  https://learn.microsoft.com/en-us/azure/architecture/
  Offers reference architectures, design patterns, and scenario-based guidance.

- **Azure**   **Policy**   **Definitions**
  https://learn.microsoft.com/en-us/azure/governance/policy/samples/
  Repository of ready-to-use Azure Policy definitions to enforce governance.

Microsoft Learn Paths and Modules

Microsoft Learn provides free, interactive training modules tailored to different roles and experience levels.

Suggested Learning Paths

- **Secure**   **and**   **isolate**   **access**   **to**   **your**   **Azure**   **resources**
  Covers   NSGs,   ASGs,   firewalls,   and   service   endpoints
  https://learn.microsoft.com/en-us/training/modules/secure-and-isolate-network-resources/

- **Design**   **and**   **implement**   **enterprise**   **governance**   **in**   **Azure**
  Explains   management   groups,   RBAC,   policy,   and   compliance
  https://learn.microsoft.com/en-us/training/paths/design-implement-enterprise-

governance-azure/

- **Azure Networking Engineer Associate Certification (AZ-700)**
  Full learning path for one of the most in-depth networking certifications in Azure
  https://learn.microsoft.com/en-us/certifications/azure-network-engineer/

Certifications and Exams

Certifications are useful for validating knowledge and are often required in enterprise environments.

Recommended Certifications

- **AZ-700: Designing and Implementing Microsoft Azure Networking Solutions**
  Role-based certification focused exclusively on Azure networking
  Topics include routing, hybrid connectivity, VPN/ExpressRoute, DNS, WAF, and monitoring

- **AZ-305: Designing Microsoft Azure Infrastructure Solutions**
  Focuses on architecture design, including networking, storage, compute, and identity
  Recommended for solution architects

- **SC-100: Microsoft Cybersecurity Architect**
  Includes cloud security strategy, governance, and network protection techniques

- **AZ-104: Azure Administrator Associate**
  Good foundational certification for those starting with infrastructure and operations

GitHub and Open Source Repositories

Many open-source projects and Azure samples are available to accelerate development, testing, and infrastructure deployment.

Key Repositories

- **Azure Quickstart Templates**
  https://github.com/Azure/azure-quickstart-templates
  1,000+ ARM/Bicep templates including VNet, NSG, load balancer, VPN, and more.

- **Azure Bicep Examples**
  https://github.com/Azure/bicep
  Official repo with sample modules, documentation, and tooling for Bicep.

- **Azure Network Watcher Tools**
  https://github.com/Azure/azure-network-watcher-tools
  CLI and PowerShell utilities for traffic analysis and diagnostics.

- **Terraform Azure Modules**
  https://github.com/Azure/terraform-azurerm-network
  Reusable Terraform modules to provision secure, scalable Azure networking components.

Books and Whitepapers

For those who prefer in-depth, narrative-driven learning, these resources are highly recommended.

Books

- **Microsoft Azure Networking: The Definitive Guide**
  Author: Jack Lee
  A comprehensive book covering VNets, load balancers, VPN, DNS, and security in Azure.

- **Azure Infrastructure as Code**
  Author: Henry Been, Eduard Keilholz, Erwin Staal
  Covers Bicep and ARM templates with deep dives into networking patterns.

- **Designing Secure Azure Solutions**
  Microsoft Press
  Covers governance, threat protection, and secure network architecture.

Whitepapers

- **Azure Networking Topology and Connectivity**
  Deep dive into patterns like hub-and-spoke, mesh, and Virtual WAN.

- **Cloud Adoption Framework (CAF)**
  Guidance on architecture, governance, and landing zones
  https://learn.microsoft.com/en-us/azure/cloud-adoption-framework/

Online Communities and Forums

Leverage the knowledge and experience of Azure professionals around the world.

- **Microsoft Q&A (Azure Networking Tag)**
  https://learn.microsoft.com/en-us/answers/topics/azure-networking.html

- **Tech Community (Azure Networking)**
  https://techcommunity.microsoft.com/t5/azure-networking/ct-p/AzureNetworking

- **Stack Overflow (azure-networking)**
  https://stackoverflow.com/questions/tagged/azure-networking

- **Reddit: r/AZURE**
  Peer advice and case studies from professionals using Azure in production
  https://www.reddit.com/r/AZURE/

Hands-On Labs and Simulators

Practical experience is the fastest way to reinforce concepts and build real-world skills.

- **Microsoft Learn Sandbox Labs**
  Many Learn modules provide temporary Azure environments for real-time labs.

- **Azure Dev/Test Labs**
  https://azure.microsoft.com/en-us/services/devtest-labs/
  Allows creation of test environments with network isolation and automation.

- **Cloud Academy / A Cloud Guru**
  Paid platforms with interactive labs covering networking, security, and architecture.

- **GitHub Codespaces + Bicep**
  Build and test Azure Bicep modules in GitHub-hosted VS Code environments.

Recommended Practice Projects

To put your knowledge to use, try building and deploying these projects in a lab or sandbox environment:

1. **Build a Secure Hub-and-Spoke Network with Firewall and Private Link**

2. **Create a Multi-Region SaaS Application with Front Door and App Gateway**

3. **Deploy a Hybrid Connectivity Lab with ExpressRoute and VPN Failover**

4. **Automate NSG and Route Table Deployment using Bicep**

5. **Simulate Network Failure Scenarios Using Chaos Studio and Traffic Manager**

Each project reinforces a specific real-world use case and builds muscle memory for critical configuration tasks.

Summary

The journey to mastering Azure networking is ongoing. With new features, architectural patterns, and compliance frameworks continuously emerging, staying current is both a challenge and a necessity. These resources—official, community-driven, and experiential—offer a diverse and comprehensive toolkit to expand your skills.

Whether you're preparing for certification, optimizing production workloads, designing enterprise infrastructure, or just getting started, these references will guide you toward deep, practical, and actionable expertise in Azure networking. In the next section, you'll find ready-to-use code snippets and sample projects to accelerate your implementation and experimentation.

Sample Projects and Code Snippets

Practical implementation is the fastest route to mastering Azure networking. This section provides detailed sample projects and code snippets that reflect real-world scenarios covered throughout the book. Each project is designed to reinforce key Azure networking concepts including virtual networking, security, hybrid connectivity, high availability, automation, and performance optimization.

You can treat these projects as standalone lab exercises or adapt them into broader enterprise environments. Each project includes a brief description, core components, and example configuration using Azure CLI, PowerShell, or Bicep. These are intended to be modified and extended to fit your learning or operational requirements.

Project 1: Secure Hub-and-Spoke Network Topology

Objective: Deploy a hub-and-spoke architecture with centralized firewall, DNS, and logging using Bicep or CLI.

Components:

- 1 Hub VNet (`10.0.0.0/16`)

- 2 Spoke VNets (10.1.0.0/16, 10.2.0.0/16)
- Azure Firewall in hub subnet
- VNet Peering from each spoke to the hub
- User-Defined Routes (UDRs) in spokes to force traffic through firewall

Bicep Snippet – Hub VNet and Firewall:

```
resource vnetHub 'Microsoft.Network/virtualNetworks@2021-05-01' = {
  name: 'HubVNet'
  location: location
  properties: {
    addressSpace: {
      addressPrefixes: ['10.0.0.0/16']
    }
    subnets: [
      {
        name: 'AzureFirewallSubnet'
        properties: {
          addressPrefix: '10.0.1.0/24'
        }
      }
    ]
  }
}

resource fw 'Microsoft.Network/azureFirewalls@2021-05-01' = {
  name: 'HubFirewall'
  location: location
  properties: {
    sku: {
      name: 'AZFW_VNet'
      tier: 'Standard'
    }
    ipConfigurations: [
      {
        name: 'fw-ipconfig'
        properties: {
          subnet: {
            id: '${vnetHub.id}/subnets/AzureFirewallSubnet'
          }
```

```
        publicIPAddress: {
          id: fwPublicIP.id
        }
      }
    }
  ]
}
}
```

Project 2: Deploying a Multi-Region App Gateway with Front Door

Objective: Deploy a global application with regional high availability and intelligent routing using Azure Front Door and Application Gateway.

Components:

- Two regional VNets (East US, West Europe)

- Application Gateway in each region with WAF

- Azure Front Door with backend pools for each App Gateway

- Health probes and geo-routing

CLI Snippet – Create Front Door Profile and Add Backends:

```
az network front-door create \
  --name MyGlobalFrontDoor \
  --resource-group GlobalRG \
  --backend-pool globalPool \
  --accepted-protocols Http Https \
  --backend-address appgateway-east.contoso.com \
  --backend-host-header appgateway-east.contoso.com

az network front-door backend-pool backend add \
  --front-door-name MyGlobalFrontDoor \
  --resource-group GlobalRG \
  --pool-name globalPool \
  --address appgateway-west.contoso.com \
  --host-header appgateway-west.contoso.com
```

Project 3: Hybrid Connectivity Lab with ExpressRoute and VPN Failover

Objective: Implement a hybrid network with ExpressRoute primary and VPN failover using Azure Virtual WAN.

Components:

- ExpressRoute circuit via provider
- Site-to-site VPN to the same VNet
- ExpressRoute Gateway and VPN Gateway in active-standby configuration
- BGP route preference setup for automatic failover

PowerShell Snippet – Configure BGP and Gateway Transit:

```
New-AzVirtualNetworkGatewayConnection -Name "ERConnection" `
  -ResourceGroupName "MyResourceGroup" `
  -Location "EastUS" `
  -VirtualNetworkGateway1 $vnetGw `
  -PeerId $erCircuit.Id `
  -ConnectionType ExpressRoute `
  -EnableBGP $true
```

This setup provides robust redundancy across hybrid links with seamless routing failover using BGP.

Project 4: Automated NSG and UDR Deployment with Bicep

Objective: Automate the deployment of NSGs and route tables with reusable Bicep modules.

Components:

- One NSG with standard rules
- One UDR to force internet-bound traffic through Azure Firewall
- NSG and UDR linked to a subnet

Bicep Snippet:

```
resource nsg 'Microsoft.Network/networkSecurityGroups@2021-05-01' = {
  name: 'MyAppNSG'
```

```
  location: location
  properties: {
    securityRules: [
      {
        name: 'AllowHTTPS'
        properties: {
          protocol: 'Tcp'
          sourcePortRange: '*'
          destinationPortRange: '443'
          sourceAddressPrefix: '*'
          destinationAddressPrefix: '*'
          access: 'Allow'
          direction: 'Inbound'
          priority: 100
        }
      }
    ]
  }
}

resource routeTable 'Microsoft.Network/routeTables@2021-05-01' = {
  name: 'MyUDR'
  location: location
  properties: {
    routes: [
      {
        name: 'RouteToFirewall'
        properties: {
          addressPrefix: '0.0.0.0/0'
          nextHopType: 'VirtualAppliance'
          nextHopIpAddress: '10.0.1.4'
        }
      }
    ]
  }
}
```

Project 5: Secure PaaS Access Using Private Endpoints

Objective: Deploy Azure SQL and Storage Account with Private Link and Private DNS for secure access.

Components:

- Azure SQL Server with Private Endpoint
- Azure Storage Account with Private Endpoint
- Private DNS zones for resolution
- Centralized DNS forwarding and zone links

CLI Snippet – Private Endpoint and DNS Zone Link:

```
az network private-endpoint create \
  --name SqlPrivateEndpoint \
  --resource-group MyRG \
  --vnet-name MyVNet \
  --subnet MySubnet \
  --private-connection-resource-id $sqlResourceId \
  --group-id sqlServer

az network private-dns zone create \
  --resource-group MyRG \
  --name privatelink.database.windows.net

az network private-dns link vnet create \
  --resource-group MyRG \
  --zone-name privatelink.database.windows.net \
  --name MyDNSLink \
  --virtual-network MyVNet \
  --registration-enabled false
```

Project 6: Custom Monitoring and Alerting for Network Anomalies

Objective: Create Log Analytics queries and alerts for key network events like denied flows, high latency, or DNS resolution issues.

Sample Kusto Query – NSG Denied Flows:

```
AzureDiagnostics
| where Category == "NetworkSecurityGroupFlowEvent"
| where action_s == "Deny"
```

```
| summarize count() by bin(TimeGenerated, 5m), src_ip = SourceIP_s,
dst_port = DestinationPort_s
```

Use this to create alerts or dashboards that surface anomalous traffic patterns in real time.

Project 7: Performance Testing with Azure Load Testing

Objective: Stress test a backend service behind App Gateway to validate autoscaling and latency under load.

Workflow:

1. Deploy   backend   API   (App   Service   or   AKS)

2. Configure   Azure   Load   Testing   with   test   plan

3. Define   thresholds   for   response   time   and   failure   rates

4. Use   autoscale   to   validate   performance   response

CLI Snippet – Create Load Test:

```
az load test create \
  --resource-group MyRG \
  --name ApiLoadTest \
  --location eastus \
  --resource-type microsoft.insights/components \
  --test-name backendstress \
  --test-plan-url
https://storage.blob.core.windows.net/loadtests/mytestplan.jmx
```

Project 8: Network Policy and Compliance Audit

Objective: Validate network resource compliance using Azure Policy and remediation scripts.

Strategy:

- Use policy definition to audit NSG rules, public IPs, route tables

- Trigger   remediation   via   Azure   Automation

- Export compliance report weekly to storage or email

Sample Policy: Deny Public IP on NICs

```
{
  "if": {
    "field":
"Microsoft.Network/networkInterfaces/ipConfigurations.publicIpAddres
s.id",
    "exists": "true"
  },
  "then": {
    "effect": "deny"
  }
}
```

Summary

These projects represent a hands-on continuation of the lessons and principles discussed throughout this book. Each one is designed to deepen your skills, expose you to new tools and patterns, and provide reusable assets for real-world environments. Whether you're building a secure hybrid network, implementing global application delivery, or developing automated governance, these projects offer tangible and immediate ways to apply what you've learned.

In the next appendix, we provide an API reference guide covering key networking resources and operations for integration, automation, and programmatic management of your Azure networking estate.

API Reference Guide

As cloud networking infrastructure becomes increasingly dynamic and automated, direct interaction with Azure services via APIs has become essential for developers, DevOps engineers, and network administrators. Azure provides RESTful APIs for all networking services, enabling full lifecycle management—provisioning, configuration, monitoring, and decommissioning—via code.

This section serves as a reference guide for key Azure Networking APIs, with focus on the most commonly used services, endpoints, request structures, and examples for authentication and automation. The guide is structured by service, providing clarity for both script-based automation and advanced integration scenarios.

Authentication and Access

Before accessing Azure APIs, you must obtain a valid bearer token using Azure Active Directory (Azure AD).

Acquire Token (Client Credentials Flow)

```
POST https://login.microsoftonline.com/{tenantId}/oauth2/v2.0/token
Content-Type: application/x-www-form-urlencoded

client_id={clientId}
&scope=https%3A%2F%2Fmanagement.azure.com%2F.default
&client_secret={clientSecret}
&grant_type=client_credentials
```

The returned `access_token` is used in subsequent API calls:

```
Authorization: Bearer eyJ0eXAiOiJKV1QiLCJh...
```

Core Networking API Endpoints

All Azure resource operations go through the base management endpoint:

```
https://management.azure.com/
```

All requests must include the API version, typically as a query parameter:

```
?api-version=2021-05-01
```

Virtual Network (VNet)

List All VNets in a Subscription

```
GET
/subscriptions/{subscriptionId}/providers/Microsoft.Network/virtualN
etworks?api-version=2021-05-01
```

Create a VNet

```
PUT
/subscriptions/{subscriptionId}/resourceGroups/{rg}/providers/Micros
oft.Network/virtualNetworks/{vnetName}?api-version=2021-05-01
```

```json
{
  "location": "eastus",
  "properties": {
    "addressSpace": {
      "addressPrefixes": ["10.0.0.0/16"]
    },
    "subnets": [
      {
        "name": "default",
        "properties": {
          "addressPrefix": "10.0.0.0/24"
        }
      }
    ]
  }
}
```

Network Security Groups (NSGs)

Get NSG Details

```
GET
/subscriptions/{subscriptionId}/resourceGroups/{rg}/providers/Micros
oft.Network/networkSecurityGroups/{nsgName}?api-version=2021-05-01
```

Add NSG Security Rule

```
PUT
/subscriptions/{subscriptionId}/resourceGroups/{rg}/providers/Micros
oft.Network/networkSecurityGroups/{nsgName}/securityRules/AllowHTTPS
?api-version=2021-05-01
```

```json
{
  "properties": {
    "protocol": "Tcp",
    "sourcePortRange": "*",
    "destinationPortRange": "443",
    "sourceAddressPrefix": "*",
    "destinationAddressPrefix": "*",
    "access": "Allow",
    "priority": 100,
```

```
    "direction": "Inbound"
  }
}
```

Azure Firewall

Get Firewall Configuration

```
GET
/subscriptions/{subscriptionId}/resourceGroups/{rg}/providers/Micros
oft.Network/azureFirewalls/{firewallName}?api-version=2021-05-01
```

Add Firewall Application Rule

```
PUT
/subscriptions/{subscriptionId}/resourceGroups/{rg}/providers/Micros
oft.Network/azureFirewalls/{firewallName}/applicationRuleCollections
/{ruleName}?api-version=2021-05-01
```

```
{
  "properties": {
    "priority": 100,
    "action": { "type": "Allow" },
    "rules": [
      {
        "name": "AllowWeb",
        "protocols": [
          { "protocolType": "Https", "port": 443 }
        ],
        "sourceAddresses": ["10.0.0.0/24"],
        "targetFqdns": ["*.contoso.com"]
      }
    ]
  }
}
```

Application Gateway

List All App Gateways in a Resource Group

```
GET
/subscriptions/{subscriptionId}/resourceGroups/{rg}/providers/Micros
oft.Network/applicationGateways?api-version=2021-05-01
```

Enable HTTP/2

```
PATCH
/subscriptions/{subscriptionId}/resourceGroups/{rg}/providers/Micros
oft.Network/applicationGateways/{appGatewayName}?api-version=2021-
05-01
```

```
{
  "properties": {
    "enableHttp2": true
  }
}
```

Public IP Addresses

Create a Standard Public IP

```
PUT
/subscriptions/{subscriptionId}/resourceGroups/{rg}/providers/Micros
oft.Network/publicIPAddresses/{ipName}?api-version=2021-05-01
```

```
{
  "location": "eastus",
  "properties": {
    "publicIPAllocationMethod": "Static",
    "sku": {
      "name": "Standard"
    }
  }
}
```

Private Link and Private Endpoints

Create Private Endpoint

```
PUT
/subscriptions/{subscriptionId}/resourceGroups/{rg}/providers/Micros
oft.Network/privateEndpoints/{peName}?api-version=2021-05-01

{
  "location": "eastus",
  "properties": {
    "subnet": {
      "id":
"/subscriptions/{subscriptionId}/resourceGroups/{rg}/providers/Micro
soft.Network/virtualNetworks/{vnetName}/subnets/{subnetName}"
    },
    "privateLinkServiceConnections": [
      {
        "name": "myConnection",
        "properties": {
          "privateLinkServiceId": "{resourceId}",
          "groupIds": ["blob"],
          "requestMessage": "Access for storage"
        }
      }
    ]
  }
}
```

Azure DNS

Create a Private DNS Zone

```
PUT
/subscriptions/{subscriptionId}/resourceGroups/{rg}/providers/Micros
oft.Network/privateDnsZones/{zoneName}?api-version=2020-06-01

{
  "location": "global"
}
```

Link a VNet to a Private DNS Zone

```
PUT
/subscriptions/{subscriptionId}/resourceGroups/{rg}/providers/Micros
```

```
oft.Network/privateDnsZones/{zoneName}/virtualNetworkLinks/{linkName
}?api-version=2020-06-01

{
  "location": "global",
  "properties": {
    "virtualNetwork": {
      "id":
"/subscriptions/{subscriptionId}/resourceGroups/{rg}/providers/Micro
soft.Network/virtualNetworks/{vnetName}"
    },
    "registrationEnabled": false
  }
}
```

Monitoring and Alerts

List Metric Definitions for a Network Resource

```
GET
/subscriptions/{subscriptionId}/resourceGroups/{rg}/providers/Micros
oft.Network/networkSecurityGroups/{nsgName}/providers/microsoft.insi
ghts/metricDefinitions?api-version=2018-01-01
```

Create a Log Analytics Workspace

```
PUT
/subscriptions/{subscriptionId}/resourceGroups/{rg}/providers/Micros
oft.OperationalInsights/workspaces/{workspaceName}?api-version=2020-
08-01

{
  "location": "eastus",
  "properties": {
    "sku": {
      "name": "PerGB2018"
    },
    "retentionInDays": 30
  }
}
```

Azure Resource Graph (for Discovery at Scale)

You can use Azure Resource Graph to query networking resources across all subscriptions:

Query All Public IPs

```
Resources
| where type == "microsoft.network/publicipaddresses"
| project   name,   location,   properties.ipAddress,   sku.name,
properties.publicIPAllocationMethod
```

API Automation Tools

You can manage Azure networking APIs programmatically using:

- **Azure   SDKs   (Python,   .NET,   Java,   JS)**
  Example: azure-mgmt-network   for   Python

- **Terraform   Provider: azurerm**
  Fully   supports   all   networking   services   via   HCL

- **Azure   CLI   and   PowerShell**
  Wrapper   around   REST   APIs—great   for   scripting   and   CI/CD

- **ARM   and   Bicep**
  Declarative   automation   using   native   Azure   deployment   templates

Summary

This API reference guide gives you a structured starting point for automating and integrating Azure network services into your own infrastructure-as-code pipelines, management tools, and cloud-native applications. With direct API access, you can perform fine-grained operations, scale deployments, implement governance at scale, and build highly responsive operational workflows.

In the final appendix, you'll find a collection of frequently asked questions (FAQs) compiled from readers and cloud professionals that address common pitfalls, myths, and troubleshooting strategies in Azure networking.

Frequently Asked Questions

Navigating Azure networking involves both strategic planning and deep technical execution. As engineers and architects work through various deployments, common questions arise around best practices, configuration nuances, troubleshooting, cost control, and platform limitations. This FAQ section distills these questions and provides detailed answers, helping to clear up confusion, prevent misconfigurations, and accelerate adoption.

These answers draw on real-world experience across enterprises, government, and startup contexts, and are applicable whether you're managing production systems or developing proof-of-concept environments.

General and Design

Q: What is the best network topology for a medium to large enterprise?

A: The **hub-and-spoke** model is recommended for most enterprises. It allows centralization of shared services (DNS, firewall, Bastion), simplifies routing, and enforces a security perimeter. VNets are deployed per workload or environment (e.g., dev, test, prod) and peered back to a shared hub. Combine this with Azure Firewall or NVAs and optionally a Virtual WAN for global scale.

Q: When should I use Azure Virtual WAN instead of manual peering?

A: Use **Virtual WAN** when you:

- Need to scale to **many VNets across regions**
- Want to simplify **hub-and-spoke automation**
- Plan to integrate **ExpressRoute, VPN, and SD-WAN**
- Need **automated route propagation** and policy

For smaller deployments or highly customized routing, manual VNet peering offers more control.

Q: Is it safe to allow internet access directly to VMs via public IPs?

A: No. Use **Azure Bastion** for secure remote access or jumpbox VMs behind NSGs. If public IPs must be used (e.g., for a web app), place the VM behind a Load Balancer or Application Gateway, apply NSG rules strictly, and enable Azure DDoS Protection and Just-In-Time (JIT) access.

Q: What address space should I assign to VNets and subnets?

A: Plan address spaces using **CIDR blocks** to avoid overlap:

- VNet: /16 (e.g., 10.0.0.0/16)

- Subnets: /24 or /27 depending on the resource count Avoid overlapping ranges with on-prem environments to prevent routing issues when hybrid connectivity is added later.

Security

Q: What's the difference between NSGs, ASGs, and Azure Firewall?

- **NSGs:** Stateless traffic filtering at the subnet/NIC level

- **ASGs:** Logical groups for simplifying NSG rules

- **Azure Firewall**: Stateful L3-L7 filtering with logging, DNAT/SNAT, and Threat Intelligence

Use NSGs for basic microsegmentation, ASGs for rule management, and Azure Firewall for advanced inspection and centralized control.

Q: How do I prevent data exfiltration from Azure resources?

A:

- Deny outbound internet access with NSG or UDR

- Use **Private Link** to access Azure PaaS securely

- Restrict traffic using **Azure Firewall FQDN rules**

- Enable **DNS Proxy** and filter external resolution

- Monitor outbound traffic with Flow Logs and Sentinel

Q: Is network isolation enough for multi-tenancy?

A: No. Combine network isolation with:

- Azure AD tenant isolation or RBAC segmentation
- Key Vault and storage access via identity-based policies
- Custom DNS zones and routing
- Application-level multi-tenancy (e.g., data filters, tokens)

Performance

Q: How can I reduce latency between Azure regions?

A:

- Use **Global VNet Peering** instead of VPN over public internet
- Deploy services in **paired regions** for optimal replication
- Use **Azure Front Door** or **Traffic Manager** for geo-routing
- Enable **Accelerated Networking** on supported VM SKUs
- Keep latency-sensitive traffic within the same region or zone

Q: Why is my Azure SQL database access slower over Private Link?

A: Check:

- DNS resolution (ensure correct private DNS zone)
- Routing (make sure UDRs don't block traffic)
- Whether clients are in the **same region**
- If clients use **forced tunneling**, optimize firewall rules to avoid unnecessary hops

Q: What tools are available to test network connectivity?

A:

- **Network Watcher**: Connection Monitor, IP flow verify
- **NSG Flow Logs** + Log Analytics
- **az network watcher test-connectivity**
- Packet capture at NIC level
- Azure Load Testing (for throughput testing)

Monitoring and Logging

Q: What are the best practices for monitoring network traffic?

A:

- Enable NSG Flow Logs and store in **Log Analytics**
- Use **Azure Firewall logs** for app-layer visibility
- Collect metrics from **Application Gateway** and **Front Door**
- Aggregate data with **Sentinel** for threat analysis
- Use **Azure Workbooks** to visualize flows and anomalies

Q: How do I troubleshoot DNS resolution issues in Azure?

A:

- Use `az network watcher dns-resolve`
- Validate DNS zone links for **Private DNS**
- Use conditional forwarding if custom DNS is used
- Enable **DNS Proxy** in Azure Firewall or NVA
- Monitor with logs from **Diagnostic Settings** on DNS zones

Automation and Governance

Q: Should I use Bicep or Terraform for infrastructure deployment?

A: Both are valid. Use:

- **Bicep** for native Azure support, best alignment with ARM
- **Terraform** for multi-cloud, modular designs, or complex workflows

Pick based on team familiarity and ecosystem integration (e.g., Azure DevOps vs. GitHub Actions).

Q: How do I enforce consistent networking standards across teams?

A:

- Use **Azure Policy** to enforce NSG, SKU, and subnet rules
- Create **policy initiatives** for resource tags, IP naming, and diagnostics
- Apply policies at the **management group** level
- Use **Blueprints** (or deploy landing zones) for large orgs

---

Q: Can I automatically disable unused public IPs?

A: While Azure doesn't disable them automatically, you can:

- Use **Azure Monitor** to detect low-usage IPs
- Write an Azure Automation runbook or Logic App to deallocate or alert
- Tag public IPs with ExpiresOn or Owner to aid review

Cost and Optimization

Q: How do I reduce Azure networking costs?

A:

- **Use Private Link** instead of service endpoints with NSG egress
- Limit **cross-region** **data** **transfer**
- Use **Azure CDN** or **Front Door** to cache content
- Review **public IP SKUs**—Basic is cheaper than Standard (but has fewer features)
- Monitor **egress costs** with Cost Analysis and custom tags

---

Q: Are inbound and outbound traffic charged the same?

A: No.

- **Inbound (ingress)** traffic is generally free
- **Outbound (egress)** is billed per GB and increases by region distance Cross-region and internet egress can accumulate costs fast.

Q: Is Azure DDoS Protection worth the cost?

A: For production and public-facing workloads, yes. Benefits include:

- SLA-backed protection
- Real-time mitigation
- Rich telemetry and mitigation reports
- Integration with Azure Sentinel
- Cost protection for attack-related egress

Troubleshooting

Q: My VM can't access the internet—what should I check?

A:

1. Is there a valid public IP or NAT Gateway attached?

2. Are NSG outbound rules allowing internet (0.0.0.0/0)?

3. Is there a UDR forcing traffic through a firewall?

4. Is DNS resolving correctly?

5. Has a firewall policy or custom route blocked traffic?

Q: I created a Private Endpoint, but the service is still using public access. Why?

A:

- Check **DNS resolution** on the client VM
- Ensure **Private DNS Zone** is linked to the correct VNet
- Make sure `privateEndpointNetworkPolicies` is disabled on the subnet
- Validate traffic is routed internally, not to the public endpoint

---

Q: VNet peering is configured but traffic isn't flowing—why?

A:

- Verify NSG rules allow required traffic
- Ensure **"allow forwarded traffic"** is enabled if transit routing is required
- Check UDRs that may override the system routes
- Validate effective routes using `az network nic show-effective-route-table`

Summary

These frequently asked questions cover a wide range of Azure networking challenges—from planning and security to automation, performance, and cost control. They reflect both common scenarios and subtle issues that emerge in real-world environments.

Keep this section handy as you architect, deploy, monitor, and troubleshoot networks in Azure. The most effective engineers combine book knowledge with continuous learning and sharp diagnostic skills—these FAQs are intended to sharpen both.